Parents are Forever

a step-by-step guide to becoming successful co-parents after divorce

Shirley Thomas, Ph.D.

Parents Are Forever: A Step-By-Step Guide to Becoming
Successful Co-Parents After Divorce

Third Printing 1997
© 1995 Shirley Thomas
All rights reserved
Printed in the United States of America

Springboard Publications
P.O. Box 484
Longmont, Colorado 80501-484

Cover and text design: Apropos Graphics
Edited by Dorothy Rankin

Library of Congress Catalog Card Number 94-73653

ISBN 0-9646378-2-0

For my children

ACKNOWLEDGEMENTS

I wish to thank my colleagues for their insights about families, divorce, psychology, and law, especially Mark Vlosky, Cathy Wimmershoff, Nick Wimmershoff, Robert Hancock, and Rod Felzein. A special acknowledgement is made to Carla Garrity and Mitch Baris for their creative work on developmental levels and parenting time patterns, which forms the basis for Step 10. Finally, I extend my gratitude to Dorothy Rankin, Darlene Reider, and Jane Brewer for their respective contributions of talent, patience, and enthusiasm.

TABLE OF CONTENTS

• Introduction

For more than twenty years I have been helping people with their parenting after divorce. In my child psychology practice I have had thousands of sessions with parting spouses—meeting them singly, with each other, or with the entire family present. Over and over I have listened to separated parents speak about the pain they feel for their children and have empathized with their anguish.

Despite my good intentions as a therapist, mediator, and family evaluator, I continue to be asked to testify in court on behalf of the children. No matter how many meetings I have or how many recommendations I make, spouses continue to disagree. Eventually I concluded that divorce presents such deep emotional trauma that even mature adults going through it become alarmingly disorganized. Although they love their children, they are often unable to set up realistic new lives for themselves or for their sons and daughters.

In spite of most parents' efforts to move forward and accept the loss of the marriage, too many still need the outside help of our domestic court system to decide how their children will be cared for after divorce. Often even after the court has intervened, parents continue to fight, and children continue to suffer.

Recently those of us in the mental health field have seen a fundamental attitude change that ultimately will help parting spouses maintain a more positive relationship until the children are grown. Terms like **"co-parent,"** meaning parenting together, are appearing more frequently—replacing other terms such as **"sole custodian,"** which implies unilateral single parenting.

This change in thinking, though, is still new to our culture. Now experts need avenues for getting information to all parents about how conflict-driven divorce hurts children and about how divorce with less conflict can help. Aids such as this book, if made available to those faced with the task of re-structuring their families, will help parents stop causing so much emotional damage to their children.

Every parent should be told that children need not be scarred forever by divorce. Current studies document the happiness of young adults reared in healthy, though divorced, families. Children cared for in an atmosphere of harmony and cooperation grow up to be well-adjusted even with the challenge of having lived in two homes. In *Parents are Forever* I draw on my professional experience as well as my personal journey as a co-parent to encourage peace and better living.

WHO SHOULD READ THIS BOOK

This manual is intended for all separated adults who are rearing children when another adult is legally designated as a caretaker. This includes not only divorcing parents but also parents who never married, grandparents, foster parents, or legal guardians. Though no book could be a panacea for curing all problems of divorce and separation, one that guides parents in the right direction can help. This step-by-step plan demonstrates how key adults in the child's life should be able to work together better.

In spite of my enthusiasm about shared parenting, I must extend an important word of caution. In a small minority of cases the practical aspects of co-parenting cannot be exercised. When the safety of a child or one parent is jeopardized by violent behavior or abuse by the other parent, outside authorities—police, mental health experts, or the court—must intervene. Usually in these families, the healthier, more competent parent eventually is assigned the entire job of caretaking, and the other parent will have limited participation. *Parents are Forever* will still benefit single parents who assume sole child-care responsibility by increasing their insight to the world of children.

HOW TO USE THIS BOOK

This book is primarily a parenting guide, but it is also a book about *recovery*. Those of you who are adjusting well to your separation may find yourselves moving quickly through Parts I and II in order to get to Part III, which is specific and direct about dividing parenting time and arranging other aspects of your child's new life.

The most valuable way to use this book, however, is to read it from beginning to end. Parts I and II outline the basis for the negative feelings that are felt in varying degrees by almost every separated mother and father. If you go through the steps in progression they will help you see why the most important task you have ahead is to learn to get along with your former partner.

Every separating parent should read the final portions of this guide. Part IV will help you follow up on your hands-on work of Part III, and the concepts will help you keep your new perspective. The steps reassure you that even if you continue to struggle with difficulties in your post-divorce family, there will be ways to tackle problems.

When you have finished *Parents are Forever* you will have increased confidence that you *can* make the future better for your child.

• Part 1 ADDRESSING THE PROBLEM OF THE PARENT-DIVORCE

If you are a loving parent facing divorce, your best efforts will be made by helping yourself adjust before you try to help your child. The reason to start with personal work is that debilitating emotions always surround separation; they cloud the future for even the strongest of individuals and make it hard to know what to do.

The first four steps of Part I take you through the emotional process of divorce from a parent's point of view. They guide you toward your own grief recovery and promote healing of your personal wounds. Most importantly, they encourage you to see why, after divorce, you will need to continue a positive parenting relationship with your former spouse for the duration of your son's or daughter's childhood. These steps lay the groundwork for successful co-parenting.

Step 1 RECOGNIZING THE PARENT-DIVORCE AS A LOSS

Divorce is a traumatic experience, much like the death of a loved one. Though statistics tell us that roughly half of all married adults eventually go through it, the end of a relationship intended to be permanent is devastating. In every case there is sadness, anger, and fear. Those who deny these emotions or pretend they are immune to them are only using unrealistic defenses to ward off the pain.

Divorce is a loss, like death, because when couples separate, the family they planned to have forever is gone. And divorce, like death, requires grieving to recover. Elisabeth Kübler-Ross was one of the first to outline the human grief process in her works on death and dying. By identifying five normal phases of mourning, Dr. Kübler-Ross created a springboard for understanding the divorce recovery process as well.

None of us can help the things life has done to us. They're done before you realise it, and once they're done, they make you do other things until at last everything comes between you and what you'd like to be, and you've lost your true self forever.

Eugene O'Neill

> ## Stages of grief as they relate to separation can be defined as:
>
> **Denial**—Initial lack of recognition of trauma, a refusal to "believe it is true" that you are divorcing.
> **Anger**—Resentment and blame directed at your former spouse or envy of those still together.
> **Bargaining**—Attempts to postpone the impending divorce or undo the separation.
> **Depression**—Sadness that surfaces when denial subsides and reality sets in.
> **Acceptance**—A more peaceful contemplation that overcomes the other emotions.

Since the works of Dr. Kübler-Ross, other specialists have written or lectured about grief and divorce. In fact countless self-help books and seminars have been dedicated to the spousal recovery process. The emphasis is usually on helping divorcees overcome feelings of rejection, guilt, and loneliness. The goal is to help the single adult attain a repaired self-concept and move on.

But less emphasis has been given to the parental loss which comes with divorce.

Consider this probable scenario:

It is the day of your wedding. You and your intended spouse have wonderful images of the future. You can envision a permanent home life together. Your hopes are based on building and attaining your dreams. From the outset of your marriage you have plans to live with, enjoy, and care for your future children together. You both intend to be parents, always.

Nearly fifty percent of all men and women who marry separate, and the majority of couples have children. So in addition to losing each other, almost half of all husbands and wives experience the loss of parenting together. This is the widespread problem of the **parent-divorce**.

To continue the scenario:

On the day your divorce becomes inevitable, your world as a parent changes forever. Not only are your hopes for a permanent home life gone, but your plans for your children are also jeopardized. No longer can you freely visualize yourself caring for—or even seeing—your children every day. Those images of you and your spouse parenting together forever will never materialize. Though you do not want to, you have to face the unavoidable loss incurred by the parent-divorce.

There are many different reasons that couples divorce, including countless versions of unfulfilled expectations, incompatibility, and betrayal. But all separating spouses strive for the same outcome. Men and women leave one another simply in hopes of a better life.

No matter what the precursors are to separation, once the decision to divorce is made final by even one spouse, the practical consequences for everyone are the same. After divorce your life is going to be very different than before, including your life as a parent.

UNDERSTANDING BLAME

When traumatic events take place, it is human nature to try to find the cause. Natural disasters, accidents, and severe interpersonal losses result in disorientation and confusion. In the case of divorce, spouses construct many levels of explanations to help themselves understand. But while one spouse may be more clear about the reasons than the other, explaining divorce is always hard for both because there is no physical or medical cause. Though phrases such as "let down," "tired of trying," or "need to move on," may be accurate, they have no tangible quality—and are very hard to accept.

The attempt to assign a reason for divorce, then, becomes a coping device that both spouses use to deal with their painful feelings. Whenever children are involved, parents' guilt is partially relieved when they think in certain ways. Remorseful mothers and fathers feel at least a little better when they conclude they are not "at fault," and blame the former spouse. Unfortunately, blame becomes the most serious obstruction to personal and parental recovery. It prevents moving beyond the stages of denial and anger to other necessary phases of the grief process.

GRIEF IN ADULTS

Although men and women grieve the loss of marriage in many different ways, general patterns occur. The spouse being left is usually more emotional than the spouse who is choosing to leave the relationship—and is also less ready to change. She or he may not have had the time to prepare for the shock of separation, may experience a total loss of control, and naturally react dramatically—often with anger. The spouse who is taking the lead in ending the marriage, on the other hand, will often feel more relieved, and seem more under control. Instead of feeling angry, this spouse will feel guilty and responsible, more ready to accept some of the blame.

10

Symptoms and stages of grief in divorcing adults, therefore, overlap or alternate rather than proceed in a clear linear progression, depending upon each partner's readiness to separate. Accompanying feelings of loneliness, abandonment, and rejection may come and go in *waves* of pain for months or even years. Each spouse's ability to adjust to the loss is controlled by his or her ability, or inability, to tolerate negative feelings and experience all phases of grief.

Anger and bargaining cause the most noticeable trouble when marriages end. These reactions deter the final stage of acceptance.

Anger

Some spouses become hostile or resentful right away—anger is a well-known emotion. Others try not to mourn the loss at all because negative feelings are so painful. But many individuals fighting grief focus on anger exclusively when denial gives way. Anger is more energizing than sadness or depression, and in a way more comfortable. It imparts a sense of action, of being able to do something about the loss. **Angry adults feel they are taking steps to stabilize their out-of-control experience, and this tends to make them stay angry.**

But spouses who become chronically angry and blaming are putting off facing other aspects of their grief, and are, in a sense, fooling themselves. Once one partner is truly resolved that the marriage is over, nothing can be done to retrieve it. When anger and blame predominate at the expense of other necessary grief emotions, they always make things worse.

Bargaining

Bargaining is the trickiest, most subtle grief reaction, and it can be the most troublesome of all. This dynamic is a naturally occurring delay tactic; its function is to delay the finality of painful loss.

Bargaining that slows the grieving process can surface in many ways. It may take the form of attempted reconciliation or of continuing to try to "change" so that a separated spouse will reconsider. Partners may decide to live separately while telling themselves they are still in love but cannot live together. **Many spouses simply defy acceptance by trying to be apart and together simultaneously.**

...he who remains passive when overwhelmed with grief loses his best chances of recovering elasticity of mind.
Charles Darwin

Bargaining can also appear as *negative intimacy*, where partners maintain a close but negative bond. Here anger and disagreement serve the function of keeping spouses joined in an unpleasant union. In a sense the negative feelings keep them married, though they may not see it this way. Separated spouses who fall into this counter-productive pattern tend to hurt each other repeatedly, almost purposely. Positive intimacy has become impossible but ending the relationship is still too hard.

Former lovers who continue a relationship with negative intimacy behave as though they have a right to keep on as key players in each other's lives, although they really don't. They try to control each other in a variety of unpleasant ways, making passionate emotional contact when they know they should stay away. They may spy on one another, call in the middle of the night, or give outright threats and ultimatums.

Some of you may recognize the dynamic of negative intimacy characterizing your own relationship after separation. If you do, it may help to learn that trying to cope in this unsuccessful fashion prevents both you and your former spouse from moving on. For the sake of the children you love, you should resist this pattern. Unproductive emotional bargaining in any form does not promote your divorce recovery. Negative intimacy especially prevents you from resolving your grief and getting on with your future.

GRIEF IN CHILDREN

Children go through the same phases of grief resolution as adults, and the stages also overlap. But their reactions do not take the same form as those of their parents. Children are more vulnerable and helpless. They also process their experiences differently at various levels of development.

Young children, for example, will show signs of blaming themselves and will rarely blame either parent for the break-up. In particular, children less than about eight years old react to the loss of the intact family with extreme sensitivity. They feel sad, lonely, and possibly angry, but also guilty and responsible. Boys and girls quickly conclude that their behavior has led to the separation. **Since they can be hurt so easily, children need to be told repeatedly they are not at fault for divorce.**

> Even a minor event in the life of a child is an event of that child's world and thus a world event.
>
> Gaston Bachelard,
> French scientist and philosopher

Children in early stages of development display their normal grief by crying, clinging, or refusing to accept new routines. They may have sleeping, eating, or mood problems for weeks, even months after the initial crisis. Some children display only mild symptoms and seem to take the separation in stride. Others react dramatically—these youngsters need much more reassurance because, for them, the change is very difficult.

It is almost universal that young children want their parents to reunite. The grieving stage of bargaining may set off exaggerated "good" behavior as an effort to keep parents together. But separated spouses who reconcile or even get together as a family to placate the children are making a serious error. They mislead their sons and daughters about the finality of divorce and also deceive themselves, because forced reconciliations usually do not last. **Providing a false sense of security by spending days or evenings as a family will prevent your child from accepting reality.**

Within months after a normal and permanent separation, young children given love and a chance to grieve begin to seem happier again. This adjustment occurs as new routines of the post-divorce family are set up and as the reorganized lifestyle becomes familiar. **When parents begin to heal and accept post-divorce reality, so do their children.**

Older children grieve more like adults. These youngsters may be initially sad but soon may turn to projecting anger or blame onto others. They may have loyalty conflicts, siding first with one parent, then the other, as a way of expressing anger. School-age or adolescent children may become difficult to please, manage, or control. By refusing to abide by parents' decisions, they draw attention to themselves and make unconscious attempts to keep the parents united.

Like the younger child's symptoms, though, the older youngster's adjustment problems usually become resolved as the normal crisis of divorce passes. After there has been adequate time to mourn and enough love communicated, the symptoms disappear. When older children are encouraged by parents who are learning to accept divorce themselves, they relax and regain security.

ACKNOWLEDGING THAT CONFLICT HURTS CHILDREN

Anger and other negative emotions are personal reactions to grief. Conflict, however is *not* a consequence of the normal grieving process. Conflict is an *interactional process* that comes from a struggle between opposing forces. Disagreements result when grieving spouses have different ideas about how to cope with the loss and need to express their feelings. Withdrawal, unresponsiveness, disharmony, fighting, and violence are all expressions of conflict as well as anger.

A minority of divorcing spouses work through the stages of grief with little or no interactional conflict. Both partners are able to demonstrate extreme personal maturity in spite of their natural anger. But relationships where spouses have equal coping ability are rare, and some degree of conflict characterizes most broken families.

"I hate it when Mommy and Daddy fight. I'm scared they both will die."
A five-year-old's-reaction to conflict

Even before divorce became prevalent, professionals learned that fighting between spouses had serious negative effects on children. Boys and girls reared in homes where parents battled constantly were found to be depressed and anxious. They developed problems with learning, behavior, and socialization. Eventually we came to believe that divorce represents a way to end vicious spousal power struggles and that children are better off if fighting parents separate.

Now parents in conflict no longer stay together "for the sake of the children." They leave each other instead, for their own well-being and sometimes even on behalf of a child who has been the focus of arguing. But in doing so parents create the trauma of loss for children. If intense family conflict continues even after separation, coping with the loss can be impossible.

Contemporary research shows that parent conflict *in any form* always hurts the child. This is the case from the beginning of the separation process, when one spouse begins to think about leaving, until long after divorce—even until the child is grown. Experts now have verified that children can get over the injury of divorce itself, but they cannot adjust to chronic expressions of anger, blame, and constant disapproval of the other parent. Studies are convincing, in fact, that children who have both divorce *and* ongoing family conflict to deal with are the worst off.

Conflict between parents harms children in two ways.

1. Conflict frightens children. The witnessing of traumatic events such as fighting, arguing, hostile actions, or violence elicits fear, panic, and apprehension. Emotions are contagious and transfer to other cues in the child's world. Children become emotionally upset in many ways because they cannot deal with fear.

2. Conflict teaches children to fight. Boys and girls develop life-long patterns of poor problem-solving when they copy their parents' attitudes and behavior. Modeling is a powerful form of teaching. Children learn to be aggressive and controlling themselves by observing their parents' hostility.

There is a clear correlation between a child's poor grief recovery and that of the parents after divorce. When children's normal symptoms of mourning fail to disappear in the expected period of time, it is an indication of inadequate grieving in the parents. Children who stay seriously unhappy or fearful become manipulating, controlling, or unduly withdrawn usually have parents with unresolved spousal conflict and poor communication.

The bottom line is that when anger becomes solidified as the primary personal coping defense of separating parents, neither they nor their children will heal because conflict will stay in the way.

THE PARENT-DIVORCE IS A LOSS WHICH MUST BE GRIEVED WITH RESPONSES OTHER THAN ANGER AND WITH EFFORTS TO AVOID CONFLICT

STEP 2　SHARING RESPONSIBILITY AND LETTING GO

Most marriage therapists agree that both spouses usually contribute to a marital break-up, even when only one partner decides to end the relationship. In a small minority of cases, problems are very one-sided, and responsibility should not be shared. Usually couples should share the blame willingly and see their respective roles, but sometimes they do not. It can be difficult to acknowledge one's own responsibility amidst the torrent of other painful feelings.

Counselors and separated spouses frequently hear an angry and emotionally rigid partner seem to admit to guilt, or apologize for past behavior, as if to share the responsibility. But this qualified confession is not believable for long, because projection and blame creep back in. The admission is followed by various explanations or justifications:

> *"I know I shouldn't have spent so much time away. . . but you made me feel unloved."*

> *"I know I am possessive. . . but it's only because I care."*

When divorcing partners excuse themselves in this way, they are not truly admitting their role in the break-up. Instead, they are engaging in unhealthy externalization of responsibility. Spouses who resort to excessive blame also avoid seeing counselors, consulting ministers, or talking to neutral family members. These are grieving men and women who resist the normal process of mourning, because guilt to them is intolerable.

The implication for those of you who are ending a relationship is clear. In order for you to completely recover and let go of your anger, you must *truly* own up to your contribution. You should identify and accept your shortcomings, mistakes, and weaknesses, whether you are the spouse choosing to leave or the one being left. You also will avoid the destructive defense of blame more easily if you acknowledge the strengths and positive attributes of your divorcing partner.

> She was no longer wrestling with the grief, but could sit down with it as a lasting companion and make it a sharer in her thoughts.
>
> George Eliot

Facing the truth takes courage and inner strength. But admitting your own part in the marital dissolution will speed your divorce recovery, and it will promote the well-being of your post-divorce family. As we will see throughout the remainder of this guide, the ability of divorced spouses to become successful co-parents hinges on the ability to resolve personal anger.

GETTING PAST MARITAL ISSUES

Frequently we hear one hurt partner in post-divorce conflict proclaim:

> *But the divorce IS my spouse's choice! I never even wanted it at all! What can I do about that?*

You can only accept the fact that your spouse wants to move on and realize that you have to let it happen. Even if your search for your own responsibility continues to turn up negative, you are going to have to let go.

20

Hanging on to hope when your husband or wife is gone for good only prolongs your mourning. Whenever you wish your partner would "change his mind" or fantasize that one day you will get back together, you slow the grieving process for both. This type of delay allows you to put off guilt temporarily by thinking that your lifeless relationship may somehow come alive. Such a fruitless endeavor really makes things harder for you personally, and it keeps you from being able to go forward with your parenting.

Again the parallel to death helps tell us what to do. When a friend or relative dies and the initial shock is over, it no longer matters exactly how the person passed away, only that he or she is gone. Usually by the time of the funeral, survivors have given up detailing the cause of death and have turned to dealing with their own feelings of loss. What counts by then is that those still alive can learn to carry on.

If you are among the unfortunate many to be faced with divorce, it will help to convince yourself that once your relationship has ended, it is over. Unless yours is a highly unusual circumstance, which will result in re-marriage after divorce, nothing you do will bring the intimacy back. The cause of the break-up is no longer relevant, so it is best to let go of the hurtful, marital issues and turn your thoughts to healing. Rather than focusing on ways you have been mistreated—the affairs, betrayals, or rejections—you should focus on your future, without your spouse, and you should make plans for your children's future as well.

Once your relationship has ended, it is pointless to continue searching for the cause of the failure, especially if you are searching outside yourself. One thing you can do is spend some time thinking about the *positive* aspects of the marriage—things you have learned from each other, the deep and joyful experiences, and of course, the most important consequence, your children. Although this contemplation may trigger sadness and an uncomfortable grief response, it will also give you comfort, and you will begin to feel better.

By giving up your angry, negative focus, you will reduce the level of conflict you experience with your separated spouse. When you turn to a positive focus and let yourself vocalize the good and pleasant memories of your lost relationship, you begin to allow your-self the freedom to live again and to parent with renewed energy.

LETTING GO OF THE NEGATIVE CLEARS THE PATH TO THE POSITIVE

STEP 3 PUTTING YOUR CHILD FIRST

Important decisions in life come readily for many people. As children, boys and girls come to expect they will do certain things with their lives, and as young adults they just do them. For you it may have seemed natural to pursue a career, go to college, marry, build a home, or start a family.

When serious problems threaten your family stability, however, decisions are harder to make. The trauma of impending divorce can shake the confidence of any spouse or parent. If you are the partner ending the marriage, it can be very difficult to

> The pressures of being a parent are equal to any pressure on earth. To be a conscious parent, and really look to that little being's mental and physical health, is a responsibility which most of us, including me, avoid most of the time because it's too hard.
>
> John Lennon

resolve personal issues in a way that protects your children. For those of you who did not choose to end the relationship, because the decision is made by your spouse, there are usually feelings of being *forced* to change. Many separated spouses resent having to move, work harder, live alone, or handle responsibilities without help.

The feeling of losing control, therefore, can be overwhelming to both partners, no matter which position you are in. Divorcing parents will find they can regain control by making good decisions and organizing their lives. And one decision every mother and father *must* make is to give their child, rather than themselves, top priority. Putting your children first after divorce will benefit your son or daughter in the most important ways. It also will restore a sense of purpose to your own life when you may need it the most.

But taking this step will necessitate concessions, and it will mean making sacrifices. As we will see in the following sections of this guide, former marital partners who put the needs of their children first have no choice but to face their angry feelings head on. They must learn to be flexible when working together in order to take the pressure off their children. Frequently they have to give in to each other, do things differently than they would like, and accept the fact that a former spouse will have his or her own style of parenting.

IDENTIFYING STRESS REACTIONS

Putting the needs of your child before your own will be easier if you fight the natural tendency to overreact in the early days of your separation.

It is normal for divorcing spouses to feel anxiety, even where there is little conflict. Many become over-sensitized to each other's behavior, and are at risk for using poor judgement. Common mistakes—like duplicating shopping and mishandling activity sign-ups for the children—begin to occur, and these often escalate disagreement.

In cases of more intense anxiety, estranged spouses skip work, have accidents, or miss important visits with their sons and daughters. In the most conflicted situations, parents become violent, impulsively move away, or even kidnap the children as they try to regain control.

Hurtful stress reactions happen because separating parents discover they cannot truly end their relationship. Instead they have the incredibly difficult task of *redefining* their relationship, as well as the rules and boundaries that govern the way they interact. Former spouses cannot re-structure the family quickly or easily, because at the same time they are grieving, they must move forward.

Stress responses explain why, even in responsible and previously stable families, children often do not seem to come first after separation. Sometimes even truly committed parents make mistakes. **When hurting spouses lose composure and fail to adapt, the children inevitably suffer.**

If you and your separated spouse are committed to putting your children first, you will try not to deny your grief by asserting yourselves in destructive ways. You will refrain from putting your children in the middle, using them to avoid dealing with each other. When you resist temptations to ask your child to deliver messages, tell your child the divorce is the other parent's fault, or treat your spouse angrily, you keep from tugging at your child's emotions.

Too often, when parents are not yet under control and still focused on themselves, they *do* triangulate the family. Children are caught between adults struggling with grief. And many parents still use our social system as a weapon. They fight furiously for their own rights in court instead of standing up for the child's emotional right for harmony.

Fortunately, though many go back to court, most divorcing spouses do not resort to the most extreme behaviors of running away or abduction. People who deeply love their children do not want to lose or hurt them. Mothers and fathers who have made it through the process of divorce are able to look back upon their past behavior more clearly. Often they express regret that their actions and judgements under stress were harmful to their children.

"I don't know what came over me. It wasn't like me to act on my impulses, but I did."
A recovered father of two children

ANALYZING ANGER

Cooperative caretaking after separation does not require friendship. It does require a non-emotional orientation, free of bitterness and leftover resentment. Most parting parents naturally have trouble accepting this attitude early on in the post-divorce phase. Some have the problem for months, however, or even years, because anger remains an obstacle much longer than it should.

Although we dealt with anger in both Steps 1 and 2, we need to focus on this unpleasant emotion here as well. **Nothing is more important for parents than learning to manage their negative feelings so they do not destroy all the positive efforts they make on behalf of their children.**

First, it can be helpful to recognize two basic types of anger:

Active Anger

Active anger is the overpowering, energizing negative feeling that is accompanied by rage and a sense of vindictiveness. This emotion frequently leads to responses of aggression or revenge. The expression of active anger may be physical, as in hitting, pushing, or shoving, or it may be verbal, in the form of crude language, screaming, or criticism. It may even be in legal form, as sanctioned adversarial litigation for the purpose of control or retribution.

Active anger may be understandable as an emotional reaction, but its overt display is never acceptable in the arena of the family. Hostile expressions are harmful to children during an unhappy marriage, and they are just as hurtful when parents are apart.

Studies show that children who witness—or even just "sense" — excessive ongoing anger and conflict on the parts of their parents become emotionally disturbed. Some youngsters turn to aggression themselves, developing antisocial and violent tendencies. Others become over-involved in peace-making at the expense of their own feelings because they are afraid. Children who worry about their parents' welfare grow up to be unhappy adults. Many are out of touch with their own inner selves because their emotional development has been compromised.

> Our children will not service our habits of thinking, our failures of the spirit, our wreck of the universe into which we bring new life as blithely as we do. Mostly, our children will resemble our own misery and spite and anger, because we give them no choice about it. In the name of motherhood and fatherhood and education and good manners, we threaten and suffocate and bind and ensnare and bribe and trick children into wholesale emulation of our ways.
>
> June Jordan, poet, civil rights activist

Passive Anger

Passive anger, though less obvious than active anger, can be just as injurious to children but in a slower, more indirect way. It also can be harder to counteract because it is harder to see.

Passive anger is internalized, controlled hostility, sometimes called "passive aggression." This style of handling frustration develops in response to a fear of *acting* angry. Emotions artificially controlled are still expressed in ways that may *seem* less angry, but they are really very hurtful because they still lead to conflict.

One who is passively angry may be neglectful or under-responsive. He or she may procrastinate, forget, or just not follow through on commitments. When this dynamic takes over, individuals resent feeling forced by others to behave as the others would like, and try to show they won't be controlled. Former spouses ignore requests from each other, fail to make scheduled payments, return phone calls late, or simply do not keep appointments—even with the children. And passive anger is usually cloaked in a mask of innocent forgetting or "busyness." With this defense, the angry parent, who also feels guilty, will not seem blame-worthy for its expression and will not be found "at fault."

27

As time goes by the child with a passively angry parent is also affected. Children chronically let down by parents who are late, miss visits, or fail to call become victims of depression. They see themselves as not worth their parent's time and conclude they are not important to the parent they love so much.

NEUTRALIZING ANGRY FEELINGS

Parents who *say* their children come first but fail to address their anger keep themselves deadlocked in grief. Those who divert their passion away from resentment are more able to escape the trap, and these spouses recover from divorce much sooner.

There are many ways to diffuse negative tension: write about your feelings in a journal, join a divorce transition support group, spend more time with friends and extended family, or just exercise. These activities encourage you to redirect your energy and take the focus off your anger.

But in spite of your other efforts, you or your separated spouse may get caught in patterns of poor logic that keep you entrenched in irrationality. No matter what else you may do to eliminate anger, distorted thoughts and ideas will continue to plague your recovery if you let them. **Learning to correct false conclusions about your child's other parent will greatly help.**

Simple behavioral techniques can help divorcing partners learn to think more clearly. One of these involves watching for common errors of logic often made by people under stress, and simply correcting them. Three examples will illustrate:

Overgeneralization

Divorcing partners sometimes make the mistake of using specific actions to come to general conclusions. For example, you may decide that "all" women are untrustworthy because of the deceptions of just one woman. Or you may conclude that your former spouse "never" shows concern for your child after he once forgot her birthday. Illogical conclusions like these will only make you angrier. To abate your negative emotions, avoid thinking in absolute terms of "all," "none," "always," and "never."

Mind Reading

Separating marriage partners often believe they know what the other is thinking. Anger escalates when one concludes that his or her former spouse is determined to make life miserable. A telephone call received at a strange or inopportune time, for example, may result in a false perception — "You are checking up on me. You want to know who I am with." Because separated men and women have lived together so long, they make the mistake of thinking they know all the motivations behind each other's behavior.

Catastrophizing

Anger also increases when divorcing spouses magnify the meaning of things that happen. For instance, one parent may refer to the behavior of the other in grossly exaggerated terms. If your former partner neglects to make a child support payment on time, your thought may escalate to disaster—"This is the worst thing a parent can do." In reality, unless the habit is chronic, a late payment is more an inconvenience than a catastrophe.

Parents determined to put the needs of their children before their own *must* learn to neutralize their anger, because anger leads to conflict. When you watch for these common errors you can stop yourself and substitute more reasonable, rational thoughts so you will feel less angry.

Throughout the remainder of this guide you will find other examples of how this kind of cognitive self-control will help.

PUTTING THE CHILD FIRST TAKES WORK, BUT IT ALLEVIATES THE PAIN OF DIVORCE

STEP 4 — MAKING A COMMITMENT TO CO-PARENT

The last step in addressing the parent-divorce involves committing yourself to the philosophy of **co-parenting**, which simply means parenting together.

Children need their mothers *and* their fathers involved in their lives after divorce. Boys and girls of any age suffer when they experience the loss of either parent, whether it happens through abandonment, a move away, or withholding by the other parent. The only thing that may be harder on children, in fact, is the additional witnessing of chronic conflict or fighting between adults who refuse to put the needs of the children first.

Children recovering from divorce need both parents in their lives for three important reasons:

Parents Divorce, But Children Do Not.

From the child's viewpoint, the basic constellation of the family does not change when parents decide to live apart. A simple diagram illustrates the triad of the family before divorce:

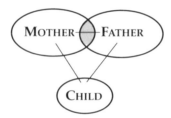

Mother and father symbols are drawn above the child to show that the parents together are in charge when the family is formed.

Both are responsible for taking care of the child, even if one parent spends more time with the child while the other works out of the home.

Spousal matters are represented in the diagram by the area of mother-father overlap. These areas of family life are not the child's business; they belong solely to the parents. Spouses' private issues include sexual intimacy, career complications, extended family problems, and financial concerns. Children should *never* be involved in marital issues, either before or after divorce. When they are, protective boundaries between parent and child become blurred, making the child worried and anxious.

The connecting lines in the diagram above stand for **parent-parent** and **parent-child** bonds of attachment. These bonds develop from the time of conception and continue through the child's life. They are built by caretaking, interaction, and routine sharing of day-to-day life by spouses and their child. Though the strength of one parent-child attachment may be stronger than that of another for any individual child, each is critical for the child's basic sense of identity.

After divorce, the family diagram may be altered to depict the estranged spousal relationship, but the lines representing the attachments—to the child and to each other—are the same.

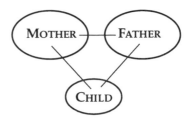

Spousal overlap and marital issues should disappear after a successful divorce adjustment. There should be no more intimacy or interest in each other's personal lives. An ongoing *parent* relationship with a former spouse will always be necessary, however, whenever a child is involved.

Sometimes, in rare cases of abuse or abandonment, maintenance of the parent-parent bond after divorce is neither feasible nor possible. By far the majority of parents who separate, however, should face the concept of "foreverness" in their own relationship. The child needs both parents to become a secure adult, even if one of the parents is imperfect or prone to making mistakes. **It is an unchanging fact that every child's reality includes both parents of his or her family of origin.**

Mothers and Fathers Parent Differently.

Historically mothers have been viewed as "softer" and more nurturing—concerned with primary caretaking duties like feeding, clothing, and bathing the children. Fathers, as major financial providers, have focused more on discipline, guidance, and recreation, adding "extras" to the child's life. Children have turned to their mothers to fill their day-to-day needs and to their fathers for support in their activities and interests.

> You don't have to deserve your mother's love. You have to deserve your father's. He's more particular. . . . The father is always a Republican towards his son, and his mother's always a Democrat.
>
> Robert Frost

Because these separate roles were perceived so rigidly for so long, fathers came to be viewed as less important than mothers, even unnecessary at times. Still, a divorcing wife often just *assumes* the primary role of parenting after separation because she questions her husband's competence to care for the children. While experts once felt this arrangement was best, few do today because the value of the father's influence is better understood.

By dividing the caretaking abilities of parents so drastically according to gender, the general population made two widespread errors. First, we underrated the nurturing potential of fathers. Now that parenting roles have become more balanced, with women working and men staying home more often, we see that fathers are able to provide excellent primary care, even for infants.

Our second error was that we overlooked the importance of the father's guidance and his interest in playing with children. Boys and girls develop optimism and high self-esteem when they laugh and play with their fathers. Now experts know that children whose fathers are not involved after divorce have fewer outside interests and feel less competent than children who see each parent frequently.

Research has documented other problems that arise when only one parent is involved. Children acquire basic skills for social interaction by relating to their parents and by watching their mothers and fathers interact with others. When either parent is left out, youngsters of both sexes seem to be less confident and to struggle with relationships. Some push themselves to relate to the opposite sex too soon, while others become delayed in social development and avoid intimacy altogether.

Boys, in general, have more obvious problems coping with divorce than girls. The reason may be that fathers disengage or are discouraged from participation in so many cases. Divorced mothers are frequently unsure about how firm to be with their son's behavior difficulties. Their lack of confidence increases as boys react with resistance, and the problems worsen over time. As a result many boys stay socially immature or become aggressive when their fathers do not see them often. They have lost the benefit of the firm male parenting that some stressed mothers cannot provide.

"My daughter is doing fine, but I just can't handle my son. He's becoming more and more disrespectful to me— almost abusive— and I really worry about him."

A mother whose former spouse is uninvolved.

Parents often observe that girls seem to have fewer problems after divorce, probably because most reside with their mothers. Women tend to be confident with their daughters, so female children display more maturity in their behavior and are more readily managed. But studies also suggest that girls who see their fathers infrequently become more depressed later on. For them, long term sadness is the direct result of losing contact with *either* parent after separation.

The important conclusion is that you should recognize the need to include both parents in the life of your child. Children benefit from the involvement of their mothers *and* fathers after divorce. **The emotional wound caused by a parent who is still alive but unavailable may fester throughout your child's developmental years, refusing to be healed.**

The Burden of Child-Care Needs to be Shared.

Divorcing parents set up a scenario for permanent harm when they try to do too much themselves and exclude the other parent. After separation the day-to-day responsibilities of each parent are at least doubled; both of you maintain complete, separate households as well as personal lives. The trials of child caretaking also become greater because of the sheer number of physical, financial, and emotional adjustments to be made.

When former spouses do not work together to share the chores of rearing their children, parental responsibilities are too often shifted to the children. Role-reversals appear, and a child's own development is quickly jeopardized. Boys assume the inappropriate role of "man of the house" when they see their mothers struggling, and girls too easily take on caretaking roles for either parent.

Children required to do too many chores or become self-sufficient too early will miss the joys of childhood.

The plain fact is that when one parent demands to take on the complete task of child-rearing alone, or almost alone, the child will suffer needlessly.

PARENTAL ALIENATION

Observations in the preceding sections show us that parting parents sometimes remain in the anger stage of mourning far longer than they should. When alienation occurs, some spouses do more than talk in negative terms about the other parent. They purposely try to exclude the other parent from the life of the child. These parents erroneously believe their *own* loss would be more manageable if they could finalize the end of the marriage by eliminating the source of the problem—the ex-spouse. Out of personal hurt and anger, they unwittingly ignore the importance of the fixed family for the child.

If you are trying to take on the sole responsibility for your child, or if you are denying your former spouse time and involvement with your son or daughter, you may be embracing an extreme form of negative intimacy, as described in Step 1. Having identified your former partner as the "problem," you may be embarking on missions to convince yourself, your child, and others that your estranged partner is a bad influence or even harmful. You may have become certain that your child would be better off seeing less of, or none of, the other parent. In your struggle to maintain a controlling link to your partner, you may discourage or disallow contact, constructing impasses and road blocks to parent time-sharing.

Divorcing parents who manifest these blind-sighted efforts to exclude each other when there is no factual basis for expecting

harm are adding to the problem. Their energy is misguided by grief and the failure to move beyond the anger stage of mourning. Separating parents who seek out flaws and dangerous behavior of the other parent inevitably hurt their children. They are attending to their own divorce recovery with self-absorption but not attending to their children's need to have both parents involved.

While there are many similarities between divorce and death, and the analogy lends certain insights, the losses are not identical. In the case of divorce, the deceased is the *relationship* you had with your child's other parent. It will be replaced with a new relationship; your former spouse in the new role of a parent living apart remains very much alive and very much to be dealt with.

Again we re-state our premise: parenting after divorce means cooperating with your former spouse so your child's family can be maintained in a reorganized, bi-nuclear way.

If you are the alienated parent or the one receiving criticism, your greatest challenge will be to maintain neutrality and refuse to enter the battle. Instead, you should continue to deal with your child in a calm and reasonable way, always reassuring her or him with your love, and always living up to your promises. In time your child will identify with your stable maturity rather than with the angry manipulations of your former spouse, and the other parent's attempts at alienation will be overcome.

FROM THE CHILD'S VIEWPOINT, *BOTH* PARENTS ARE FOREVER

•Part 2 PREPARING TO RESTRUCTURE THE FAMILY

Once you have made headway in recognizing your personal issues and have decided to get past them, you are ready to think ahead. Now you should begin to focus on the re-structured family you will become after divorce, with your child fixed at the center of the continuing parenting relationship.

Steps in this section explain what you need to know in order to prepare your child and yourself for a different kind of family life. The ideas are about how to communicate in productive ways and how to make the changes easier. Read them with an open mind so that when you reach the "hands on" steps in Part III you will be prepared to make the best arrangements possible for your child.

STEP 5 COMMUNICATING WITH YOUR CHILD

Far too often, youngsters are left in the dark when their parents divorce. In abrupt and shocking ways they find out they will be losing a parent, moving, changing schools, or losing friends. They overhear fragments of their parents' conversations, witness arguments, or otherwise just *figure out* what is happening without really being told anything at all.

Usually this troublesome lack of communication happens only because parents are too upset themselves to see that their children need to know what is happening. It is difficult for parents to face the ones they love, and they put off talking about separation. But once the children *have* been told, parents always feel a sense of relief.

TALKING ABOUT DIVORCE

Before you are certain about divorce, your children should be told only that you and your spouse are having problems. When you know for sure that you are separating, your children need to be given information and reasons that are appropriate. Explanations may need to be repeated, gently, several times in different ways. Children who are ignored while plans for separation are going on around them become unnecessarily anxious and insecure.

How you talk to your children about divorce is critical to their sense of security. Being too blunt or honest is just as bad as glossing over the problem. **The best rule is to tell your children enough so they are prepared for the change to come in their lives but not so**

"Daddy, where is Mommy? Isn't she coming home?"
A child bewildred by separation.

41

much as to frighten them. **The key to talking to children about divorce is to use neutral terms while describing the truth and avoiding the assignment of blame.**

Explaining That There Will Be a Separation

Father: *Your mother and I loved each other very much when we got married and when you were born, but now we don't feel the same. We have decided to live apart. We both love you very much though, and we will each have a home for you.*

Explaining the Reason For the Divorce

Mother: *Your father and I just don't get along like we did when you were born. We think we will be happier living apart. It's no one's fault and there's no one to blame. We both still love you very much, but we don't love each other, and we can't live together anymore.*

Explaining What Will Happen

Father: *Mother is going to be finding an apartment soon, and you and I will keep living here. There will be a special spot for you in the new apartment and a place for you to sleep. You will be taking some toys and clothes over there so you can have them with you when you spend time with Mom.*

Explaining Time-Sharing

Mother: *When parents live apart, the children still see both Mom and Dad. You will be spending time with each of us. To* start with, you will live mostly at the new apartment with me because I have taken care of you every day, for the most part. But you will be going to Dad's on Wednesdays after school to eat dinner with him before coming home to me. You will spend some weekends with Dad, too, taking turns spending weekends with me.

Reassuring The Child

Father: *Things will seem different at first, but soon you'll get used to the new schedule. I think you'll like it. Lots of children have two homes. Your mom and I want you to feel good in both your homes, so we will work together to make them nice for you.*

Responding To Difficult Questions

Child: *Mom, Dad is acting like the divorce is your fault. He seems angry and doesn't want to talk.*

Mother: *Dad may be upset because things are changing so much right now. It's ok for him to feel angry. The divorce is not my fault, but it's not your dad's fault either. It's nobody's fault. It just has to happen so we can be happier. Things will be better before long.*

Explaining That Divorce is Final

Child: *Dad, do you think you and Mom will get back together someday? Maybe if we all take a vacation like we used to, Mom will decide to marry you again.*

Father: *I know you would like us to get back together. It's natural for you to want your parents to live in the same home. But our decision to divorce is final, and your mother and I will not be living together. I think you will feel better when you see that things go well for us when we are living apart.*

The most common mistake parents make in talking with their children is to blame each other in some way. Most mothers and fathers know that blatant negative talk in the form of "bad-mouthing" is hurtful to the child, but many, unfortunately, still do it. Hearing criticism of either parent stimulates fear and anxiety in the minds of boys and girls and sets off questions about their own self-worth. Children identify with their parents—they see themselves as being similar to each of them. A child's self-esteem is quickly lowered by negative comments about either parent. **Criticizing your former spouse, therefore, is the same as criticizing your child.**

Sometimes parents are less forthright with their disapproval but still transmit criticism. Spouses unknowingly harm their children when they share intimate or private details in order to explain divorce or blame the other parent with subtle comments, such as, "It's your father who wants the divorce—not me." Explanations like these are still one-sided, no matter how well-intended. They often contain distortions and exaggerations, even misinformation.

Inappropriate adult explanations such as confiding the "truth" about one parent's affairs or indiscretions will confuse and upset even an adolescent. They also manipulate a child of any age into feeling sorry for one parent and into trying to take care of the adult.

As we saw in Step 3, parents who put the *children* first will make efforts to keep separate their own needs for emotional support.

Once more we see that responsibility for parental separation must be shared between both partners before complete recovery can occur. Nowhere is this fact more relevant than in parent-child communication.

LISTENING FOR FEELINGS

Sadness is the most common emotion felt by children during and after divorce. Many other negative feelings also surface as the child naturally goes through stages of the grieving process. Anger, fear, confusion, and guilt will all be experienced as boys and girls begin to face the reality of separation.

> But the child's sob curses deeper in the silence
> Than the strong man in his wrath!
> Elizabeth Barrett Browning

Parents can help their children deal with negative feelings by using a technique favored by child and family counselors. *Reflective listening* involves responding to your child's words or behavior so your own words encourage more expression. The benefit of this type of listening is that children begin to feel better because of the talking process itself. Although you cannot entirely protect your children from the pain caused by the family's break-up, you can help by encouraging them to say more about their feelings.

The key to reflective listening is to make responses that re-state or "mirror" the child's feelings. This lets your son or daughter know you understand. Questions or directives that stop discussion do not help because they discourage the child from talking.

The following examples show the difference between the kind of listening that does not help and the kind that does. By reading them you will see that dead-end statements or commands for the child to stop feeling a certain way are the most destructive:

Example 1

Child:	*I hate eating dinner without dad.*
Reflective Response:	*It sounds like you are angry.*
Child:	*I am. I don't like this divorce.*
Reflective Response:	*I understand that you feel bad.*

This parent mirrors the child's feelings and avoids a road-block response, such as, "Well, you had better get over your feelings."

Example 2

Child:	*I think I'll skip my time with Dad this week.*
Reflective Response:	*You don't want to see your father?*
Child:	*Oh yes I do, it's just that I have a school project to get done.*
Reflective Response:	*I see. Let's tell your dad so he knows you need time for your school work.*
Child:	*Okay. Thanks.*

This parent's response might have been, "Well you can't skip your parenting time, so just get ready to go." In such a case, the child would have felt misunderstood.

Example 3

Child:	[silence with a sad look]
Reflective Response:	*You look sad.*
Child:	*I am, kind of. I don't know why.*
Reflective Response:	*Maybe you miss your mom.*
Child:	*I do.*
Reflective Response:	*Why don't you give her a call.*
Child:	*Okay—I will.*

The parent here has successfully reflected the child's feelings and acknowledged that the child may be lonely. Gentle probing often results in the best solutions to problems.

Parents always help their children with feelings when they react slowly and with empathy without closing the door to communication. After divorce children need reassurance that they are understood and that they are loved.

CHILDREN NEED TO BE TOLD IN NEUTRAL TERMS
AND LISTENED TO WITH PATIENCE

STEP 6

FORMING A BUSINESS
RELATIONSHIP

Mothers and fathers who dissolve their marriage bond cannot truly end their relationship. Instead, once you are sure you will be separating and you have let your children know, you should start *re-negotiating* the ways you relate to each other.

Step 4 illustrated that parents after divorce maintain an association that is unlike the marital relationship. Personal issues disappear, but the parental bond between mother and father stays. The *only* reason you keep a connection is so you can conduct the business of caring for your children.

You and your former spouse demonstrate ultimate love for your sons and daughters when you willingly become business partners in parenting. Parents who work together to care for their children after divorce become *co-parents*. Neither friends nor enemies, now you are like co-workers, and you are most effective when you conduct yourselves as a parenting team.

No matter how ex-spouses may continue to *feel* about each other personally, co-parents who want to be successful *act* reasonably. They show neutral responses to each other and make sensible, logical decisions. Good co-parents avoid conflict. They control their negative emotions and express personal feelings in private—not in parent "business meetings," where common courtesy prevails. **Abuse, rude criticism, and the pursuit of personal vendettas are entirely out of order in the parenting workplace.**

The concept of the co-parent business relationship was first set forth by Isolina Ricci in her book, *Mom's House, Dad's House.* The idea is very helpful and can be easily elaborated. Parents as business partners should attend formal meetings where child-related issues are discussed. Between business meetings co-parents carry out their duties with resolve to do a good job. Remember, your child loves both of you, and nothing should interfere with that love.

Co-parents striving for excellence pick up and deliver the children promptly and do whatever is necessary to make life go smoothly for the children. They keep their agreements and follow time-sharing routines responsibly. Partners speak positively or unemotionally about the other parent, as they would about any other business associate. They try to empathize with the child's feelings so the child will not be drawn into conflict. For the sake of the children, partners in parenting should always act in good faith and work in a unified way.

BARGAINING

In Step 1 we saw that former spouses often resist ending the failed marriage in spite of their decision to divorce. They do this to avoid dealing with pain. **Bargaining** as a stage of grief is a normal deterrent to reaching acceptance of the loss, but it is unproductive. Efforts to maintain your old relationship after divorce are unrealistic, and they do not benefit your child.

With the focus on a business relationship, though, a new kind of bargaining is required. In this case the process is productive and even necessary for success. **If you and your former spouse can switch to this type of bargaining, you will diminish the effect of loss for your children and also for yourself.**

"Of course Lisa can attend your brother's wedding. I'll just see her briefly that weekend and trade the next Saturday with you."
A mother who negotiates well.

50

Healthy negotiating—with proper distance and respect for one another—is an essential ingredient for a post-divorce parenting alliance. You and your co-parent bargain productively when both of you focus on easing the pain for your sons and daughters and put their needs before your own.

Former spouses who bargain well are able to be flexible and reasonable. They go along with each other's parenting-related requests: for example, trading parenting time slots when necessary. **Through the process of cooperation, parents are able to salvage what they should of their original relationship—maintenance of the gratifying parental bond.**

Divorced parents who continue to have problems in their relationship do not bargain effectively. In many cases they continue to confuse their personal needs with those of their children. One parent may conclude, for example, that a spouse who treated him or her unjustly will also be unkind to the child. Then this parent discourages time-sharing and begins to alienate the child from the other parent. Angry mourning, unproductive bargaining, and grief have interfered with the business relationship.

When both former spouses put the needs of their children before their own by learning to bargain well, they take great strides toward recovery. After you have accepted the task of re-structuring the natural family, you even *contract* with your divorcing partner about the well-being of your child in a very

> When you look at your life, the greatest happinesses are family happinesses.
> Dr. Joyce Brothers

specific way. Appendix B of this manual presents a prototype for the kind of formalized plans and agreements parents should make on behalf of their children.

RE-FRAMING

The idea of forming a business relationship with your former spouse may seem impossible to one who is recently separated and still feeling angry and hurt. "How can I do this?" you may think. After all, if you were able to get along, you probably would still be together.

I know of no more disagreeable situation than to be left feeling generally angry without anybody in particular to be angry at.

Frank Moore Colby

One thing you can do is try to see that your own need to be negative is no more than a normal coping device. Once you understand that your reactions are not necessarily justifiable, you can begin to *re-frame* your internal responses with the same neutrality you use when talking to your child. If you tell yourself that your pessimism has a purpose for you personally but that getting past this pitfall is important, then mastering the technique of thinking neutrally will be easier.

Three examples of re-framing will show you how to control your negative thought patterns and calm yourself down.

Situation 1.

Your former spouse seems angry, hostile, and disagreeable.
Your own response may be anger or defensiveness and blame:
My spouse is a horrible, hateful person.
But after re-framing, your response can be more tempered:
My spouse is hurting right now, and this is an understandable reaction.

Situation 2.

Your former spouse is unresponsive to your requests for money and more help with the children.

Your negative thought may be:

My selfish spouse is treating me and the children terribly.

But a more rational replacement may be:

My spouse is having trouble adjusting to family changes.
I will be able to deal with this.

Situation 3.

Your child's other parent is inconsistent in keeping appointments with your son or daughter, and sometimes does not call.

A self-destructive internal response could follow:

My spouse is thoughtless and incompetent.

But a re-framed reaction might replace it:

My spouse seems to need my encouragement to become more secure and involved.

After you have repeated this type of exercise enough, you will find yourself automatically substituting neutral or positive responses for negative thoughts. The most important element is learning to view your pessimism differently so you can give it up permanently, in favor of happier, optimistic thinking.

COGNITIVE DISSONANCE

Another way of changing your own style of responding is to understand *cognitive dissonance*. An uncomfortable condition of conflict within a person can result from inconsistencies between one's beliefs and one's actions. To resolve the conflict, most people simply change their attitudes to correlate with their actions.

An individual who spends too much money on a new car, for instance, will tell us about the best, most attractive features of the vehicle to justify the exorbitant purchase. Likewise, an individual going through divorce will most likely tell us the negative qualities of the rejected or rejecting spouse. To reduce discomfort and justify your separation, you naturally describe your former spouse in negative terms. If you recognize that you have a need to view your former spouse negatively just to rationalize divorce, you will be able to minimize this tendency.

Divorcing spouses should practice re-framing and reducing cognitive dissonance in positive ways. Those who adopt a position of shared responsibility and acceptance seem to become happier sooner. **When former spouses cease voicing the faults and shortcomings of each other for the purpose of justification, they can proceed with the business of parenting together.**

REFUSALS TO CO-PARENT

An unpleasant reality is that sometimes only one parent is willing to work at co-parenting. Here the problem-parent remains stuck in the anger stage of mourning, self-absorbed, unable or unwilling to move on. He or she deals with dissonance unproductively, always blaming, criticizing, and externalizing responsibility, regardless of the healthier parent's efforts to change.

If this is your predicament, even your best attempts to co-parent in a business-like fashion will be thwarted. To your dismay and that of your child, your hurt and angry ex-spouse will continue to seize control. She or he may press for unreasonable patterns of parenting time, demand to be consulted for every minor decision, and frequently claim that his or her rights have been violated. This poor co-parent is like a poor business person who continues to derive "secondary gain," or indirect pleasure, from maintaining conflict. Forming a working business relationship with this individual seems to be impossible.

When the desire to co-parent is lopsided, the burden is even greater on the one parent who *will* adapt and who *is able* to make helpful concessions. In this case, it is paramount that the healthier parent accept and understand the goals and methods of co-parenting, rather than give up or succumb to the other parent's argumentative ways. Until things change for the better, he or she alone must make flexible decisions when faced repeatedly with the other parent's rigidity.

"I've tried every-thing. She won't even talk to me. It just makes me want to give up."
A frustrated father.

ABUSE AND DOMESTIC VIOLENCE

Another grim fact of this decade is the extent to which child and spousal abuse has come to our attention. Appalling scenarios can surface during periods of family upheaval. Even worse than the stubborn, passively angry spouse is the partner whose personal self-control is so inadequate as to allow breakthroughs of rage and violent behavior.

Domestic violence should *never* be tolerated, even in a culture promoting extensive family re-structuring and the continuing involvement of both parents. Women or men who are afraid to maintain an alliance with a threatening ex-spouse, therefore, need guidelines for determining when special safety precautions must be taken and, in the extreme, when principles of cooperative parenting should be abandoned.

Recent research on conflict in separating families reveals at least two levels of violence that appear when couples divorce. The findings are encouraging. They suggest that tendencies toward physical violence only preclude co-parenting in extreme instances. In most cases the conflict can be reduced when certain steps are taken. If you are a parent concerned about abuse in your family, it may help to review these distinctions.

Situational Divorce-Related Abuse

Earlier in this guide we listed problematic stress reactions divorcing spouses display at the time of the break-up. Violent episodes can occur as one of these symptoms, even in families with no history of such serious lack of control. Here abusiveness is really uncharacteristic of either partner's behavior. Triggered mainly by the trauma of separation, it is not a reflection of the offending spouse's permanent abusive nature.

Identifying this type of conflict helps. While temporary measures for safety may need to be taken, in these cases it is likely that the atypical behavior will subside as the crisis of divorce passes. Especially with personal counseling emphasizing the importance of the parent business relationship, the violent spouse who loves his or her children will regain control and will be able to work toward co-parenting.

Chronic Character-Related Abuse

Individuals with long histories of becoming violent have more serious psychological problems and are less able to change. **When there has been a serious pattern of abuse throughout the marriage, the offending spouse may never become a workable co-parent.**

Separating families with these dynamics will always need the outside help of courts, attorneys, or mental health professionals for guidance and protection.

Even in families where chronic violence is a problem, however, the abusive parent often has loving feelings for the child, and the child usually loves the parent as well. Maintenance of the parent-child relationship *in shielded form* is still valuable. Especially during a phase of intense treatment to determine the extent rehabilitation may be possible, some contact with the abusive parent will prevent total loss for the child.

When problems of serious violence occur, the concept of the parent-business relationship is especially important. **Supervised visitation** may be arranged by supporting professionals. To make this type of parenting time possible, both parents will be asked to follow procedures set up by others who delegate the responsibility of monitoring parent-child contact. When non-abusive parents are asked to go along with supervised visitation, the concept of co-parenting is not given up entirely but maintained in an extreme business fashion.

Though the problem of abuse is serious, the number of families who experience violence in our country is still relatively small. This means that by far most separating parents should readily adopt the cooperative premise and continue looking for progress. The worst thing a willing co-parent can do is to withdraw entirely, or lose determination to carry on.

IN EVERY CASE, CO-PARENTING IS A
BUSINESS-PARTNER RELATIONSHIP

STEP 7 STRUCTURING THE CO-PARENT MEETING

Step 7 introduces an important procedure that should become the on-going forum for making parenting decisions until your children are grown.

WHAT IS A CO-PARENT MEETING?

At the time a divorce becomes legal, the court in the state of jurisdiction must enter a plan providing for the care of the minor children. This is the Co-Parent Plan. Parents who can meet with each other and successfully make decisions will control their own parenting plans. Those who cannot because of conflict or unwilling-ness must be ultimately assisted by attorneys, evaluators, and a judge. These parents are in considerably less control of their own lives after the decree of separation is final.

When you and your spouse file for divorce, you will be able to keep the power and control out of the adversarial system if you both make the effort. As soon as you have sufficiently recovered from your own trauma and grief, you should adopt the partnership atti-tude and get on with the business of re-structuring the family. Most of your important decisions regarding your children should be made during co-parent meetings.

BEFORE THE DIVORCE IS FINAL

Committed parents should sit down together several times before the divorce agreement has been finalized in a quiet and neutral place. The purpose of the meeting is to discuss the welfare of your children and to draw up a parenting plan. You will be most successful if you learn to do this early after separation. **To postpone facing each other, even occasionally, delays divorce recovery for your child as well as for yourself.** When there is a geographical split between homes, co-parents still do well to make sure meetings take place, even if only by telephone.

Step 9 suggests that you have the Co-parent Checklist available when you meet. Step 10 outlines recommended parenting time routines for children of increasing ages and developmental levels. These tools are for your continuing use, but they are most important at the outset of your separation. In the first year after divorce you are learning to co-parent and put the needs of your child before your own. Without this information you may overlook important aspects of caretaking, or make mistakes in the way you divide parenting time.

> When two people decide to get a divorce, it isn't a sign that they 'don't understand' one another, but a sign that they have, at last, begun to.
>
> Helen Rowland

AFTER THE DIVORCE IS FINAL

Legalization of divorce does not end the parenting alliance; it marks the official beginning of your restructured relationship. As co-parents you will go forward for years in the business of caring for your children.

Co-parent meetings are a forum for ongoing communication. After a few sessions you will learn to come with your own checklist of issues that arise in your daily lives. If you follow basic procedural rules and practice techniques of negotiating, you will be successful at maintaining your parenting coalition.

When your children are young you should schedule meetings frequently. Some parents choose to meet as often as once per month, but others want fewer meetings. Newly divorced spouses, especially, often need a break from dealing with each other. Once the parenting plan is in place, it is possible to meet less frequently.

At least two meetings each year should be scheduled when your children are under six or seven years of age. You will review your children's needs and make necessary adjustments in your co-parent plan. During the school-age years you should continue to meet at least annually, or more often if problems arise. Use the neutral structure of the parent business conference every time you need a serious consultation.

RULES OF PROCEDURE

Simple rules of business procedure will help you conduct a successful co-parent meeting. The following guidelines will help all former spouses work through their worries about the children. If you both agree to use them, the rules offer a structure and basic course of action that can be turned to whenever you work together.

1. Make appointments to talk to each other. Impulsive, spur of the moment conversations are not well thought out. They often stimulate anger and poor problem resolution. When you plan to meet at a certain time and place, you will be calmer and more rational.

2. Be prepared to communicate with your co-parent. Make lists of your concerns and decide ahead of time that you are determined to work things out. Prepare yourself for success by being specific and avoiding abstract descriptions of problems. An issue listed clearly, such as "deciding how allowance will be handled," is much easier to address than one phrased vaguely, for example, "respecting our children."

3. Begin parent talks by deciding easy issues where there is already considerable agreement. Discussing harder issues will go better after success with easier ones. Most parents agree in many more areas than those in which they disagree. If you talk about some of these commonalities first you will feel much better about yourselves as business partners.

4. Take turns discussing your thoughts and stay on one topic at a time. Set limits for the amount of time each parent spends on one issue—this keeps you from getting stuck and not making progress. Learn to listen accurately by summarizing each other's points of view. Try to hear the *concern* behind your co-parent's interest in making each decision.

5. Keep past marital issues out of parental business talks. Remember, the marriage is over. Reread Step 2 of this manual. The co-parent meeting is a business session that will succeed only if you maintain neutrality and mutual respect.

6. Agree ahead of time to alert each other when marital issues begin to come up or when anger interferes. Use an identified signal to call a time-out when you need to. The verbal statement "time out" can work to help you calm down and re-focus on the needs of the children.

7. Discuss issues one-by-one and consider all your options. Be specific and thorough, then write down your decisions. Validate each other as you talk by mentioning each other's good points. Be polite and courteous, never losing the business orientation.

8. If you find you must be critical, target the idea or proposal instead of the other parent. Never attack your co-parent, even with sarcasm or "harmless" personal comments. Backsliding into personal issues will undermine your efforts and will make progress more difficult.

9. Table issues you cannot resolve until another time. Agree to work on difficult items between co-parent meetings by trying to find more options and present these at the next work session. Your list of disagreements will narrow quickly if you continue to look for new ways to address them.

10. End the meeting by mutual agreement or when the allotted time has run out. Never terminate talks in anger by walking out after a frustrating set-back.

NEGOTIATION
Once you have internalized the rules of procedure, you are ready to negotiate agreements.

Stages to Successful Negotiation

The process of negotiation can be divided into three stages that lead to solutions. After you have chosen an item to work on, you can follow these steps to reach agreement:

1. Define the issue. Each of you should state your concerns and your ideas about how the matter should be decided. Be as specific and exact as you can.

2. Brainstorm possibilities. The key to finding common ground is to avoid the win-lose trap by deciding "my way" or "your way." Brainstorming requires you to be creative and write down many thoughts. Continue looking for alternate plans, even those that seem unworkable at first. Later you will rule out proposals that clearly will not benefit your child. When each of you contribute *all* your ideas to begin with, you maximize your chances of finding the best result.

3. Eliminate unworkable solutions. By a process of elimination you will arrive at a mutually acceptable decision. Each of you can rule out alternatives that clearly are poor for your child. Eliminating the ideas you both reject will bring you closer to agreement. Go back to brainstorming more when choices seem too limited or when you begin to feel cornered. You and your co-parent will finally settle on a plan that allows each of you to have your concerns addressed.

One example of successful co-parent negotiation will illustrate how the process can work: **A separated mother and father are in disagreement over whether to leave a 12-year-old home alone during evening hours.**

Step 1. Define The Issue

Mother explains that she feels the child is too young and may be frightened if left unsupervised. Father explains that he feels the child is old enough to be given increased responsibility.

Step 2. Brainstorm Possibilities

Mother and father list these possibilities:
The child could always be left alone in the evening.
The child would never be left alone in the evening.
The child could be left alone at one home, but not the other.
The child could be left alone until 9 p.m. at either home.

Step 3. Eliminate Unworkable Solutions

Mother and father rule out the first three possibilities as unacceptable and settle on the 4th, which addresses the basic concern of each of them. The child will be given the responsibility of staying home alone but only until 9 p.m.

The negotiation process is not a cure-all for ending disagreement. It is a tool that can help parents deal with differing views. If you and your former spouse have adopted the business orientation and become committed to cooperation, you will be able to negotiate most areas of disagreement yourselves.

Even parents who cannot negotiate successfully or who choose not to meet formally should follow basic rules of cordial communication. Those who must send lists of concerns and proposals through the mail or through attorneys because they cannot deal with each other will eventually arrive at a plan, but the process will be more cumbersome and more costly. Once the initial parenting plan is in effect, *all* caring co-parents should go back to facing each other directly when they can, in order to put the children first.

MEETINGS BETWEEN CO-PARENTS SHOULD HAVE AGENDAS AND RULES OF PROCEDURE

• **Part 3** CREATING THE CO-PARENTING PLAN

This is the most down-to-earth part of the guide. Here you are given advice to help you focus on your child's day-to-day needs after divorce. Use the ideas to work with your co-parent and restructure your family. The Co-Parent Check-list in Appendix A can be kept on hand when you have your meetings. It will help you remember to think of items that are important in child caretaking, and will give you a place to organize your proposals. The Sample Co-parent Plan in Appendix B can be used as a prototype for completing your parenting agreement. Even if you opt for sole custody, the tone and language of the sample contract will help you see the importance of making thoughtful plans for your children.

STEP 8 LEARNING THE GUIDING PRINCIPLES

Three principles of child development are especially helpful for mothers and fathers who share parenting after divorce. You and your co-parent can refer to these guidelines when you finalize your agreements at the time of divorce and whenever you review your plan.

MINIMIZE LOSS

When separation occurs children lose the luxury of a single home with both parents present on a daily basis. This loss is unavoidable, since the child cannot live in two places at once. First, you should recognize that this loss-of-one-home is the basis for your child's mourning after divorce. In every case the child will grieve the loss of the intact natural family. No arrangements co-parents make can prevent the normal course of this grief.

Loss always triggers anxiety and grief, and because its effect after divorce is cumulative, co-parents should eliminate other unnecessary losses for their child. Children who lose everything—their contact with one parent, their primary home, their school, neighborhood, and friends—have a much greater journey to recovery.

When co-parents make an effort to keep the life of the child as much the same as possible after divorce, they serve the child well. Children of these co-parents are more relaxed and trusting, since they are able to use the security of their environment as an anchor.

MAKE SMALL CHANGES

In general, children do not adjust easily when there are large changes in their lives. Accommodating newness is harder for younger children than older children because they are developmentally more sensitive and more prone to overreact. Further, all children are born with different temperaments and individual differences. The very nature of their dispositions affects their ability to adapt. While some are low-keyed, complacent, and accepting, others are from birth high-strung, fussier, and resistant. The former may do fairly well with change, but the latter do not.

With divorce it is best to make small steps of change for your children, especially while they are young. This may mean making the child's bedrooms in both homes similar or duplicating toys so the environments will be alike. It will also mean keeping the same activities, day-care people, and friends in the daily life of your child, if you can, to prevent too much change and loss.

> Most of us are about as eager to be changed as we were to be born, and go through our changes in a similar state of shock.
>
> James Baldwin

In setting up patterns of co-parenting, the rule-of-small-change tells us that your young child will do best if life continues to be nearly the same as it was before. This includes the interpersonal world of relationships. Infants, toddlers, and preschoolers, who have only brief memory capacity and a limited sense of time, should see both their parents often. They also should live in one home, or mostly in one home.

For the very young child, under age five or so, it is best for one home to be primary and the other secondary, even when both parents are equally important and equally bonded to the child. Every young child's sense of trust and confidence in people is developed by having consistency and routine in daily care-taking. The primary residence should be with the parent who, before divorce, has cared for the child on a day-in, day-out basis.

Younger children do better with short but frequent time-share visits to the non-primary home because the amount of change required is smaller. As children grow older it becomes easier for them to accommodate larger changes, and periods of parenting time can be longer. While two-year-olds do not do well with half or full weeks away from the primary parent, many ten-year-olds do, and for them parents can consider the possibility of 50-50 residential sharing. Vacations and holidays can also be extended. In general, as children grow older, the options for acceptable parenting arrangements increase.

MAKE GRADUAL CHANGES

Children also need *time* to adjust. Giving them time for adaptation increases their mastery and sense of competence. It allows them to move on to new challenges of childhood with eagerness and receptivity. It prevents regression or resistance to new tasks of development. This is why, for example, children attend half-day kindergarten programs for a full year before moving on to first grade. Five-year-olds need time to assimilate the newness of school and to adjust to the separation from home before they graduate to full-day programs.

Similarly, children after divorce need time to adjust to going back and forth between homes. They need to internalize both environments as their own. **Children pushed to adapt too quickly by parents eager to reach a plateau of equal or near equal time-sharing may not thrive with the new regime.** Well-meaning adults, in fact, do the child a disservice when they do not allow the appropriate weeks, months, or even years for the child to adapt. Co-parents should be sensitive to the possibility that a child of any age may show adjustment problems or resist the parenting time schedule if the rule of gradualness is ignored.

Step 9 contains specific suggestions for dividing parenting time according to your child's age and developmental level. A careful look at these patterns will show that they follow the guiding principles of minimizing loss while making small and gradual changes.

UNNECESSARY LOSS AND CHANGE SHOULD BE AVOIDED

STEP 9 COMPLETING THE CO-PARENT CHECKLIST ✔

The Co-Parent Checklist in Appendix A is an inventory of caretaking topics that should be discussed at parent meetings before the divorce becomes final. Although it may not contain every concern you have for your child, it includes the most important items, and it provides a place to record your working decisions.

The items on the Checklist are those most frequently mentioned by parents after divorce, as mothers and fathers begin to think about the reality of the new family. Issues are arranged according to the approximate order in which they seem to arise. Several meetings may be necessary to get to all the topics.

You will use your decisions from the Checklist to write your parenting plan. Determinations about most of the items, and perhaps others specific to your family, should be included in your final draft. Provided that neither spouse "runs the whole show" during negotiations, the more self-made decisions you can make, the better it is. Highly detailed plans work the best—these will provide more structure so that fewer meetings are needed during the early post-divorce period.

CO-PARENT DECISIONS

The following section is a summary of suggestions and practical advice about each item on the Checklist. Ideas are compiled from the author's experience as a psychologist and from her review of writings by other professionals studying the best interests of children after divorce. At the end of the list a space is provided for you to consider issues which may be specific to your own family, such as special provisions for a handicapped child.

After reading the recommendations and talking together, you should make final decisions based on your knowledge of your own children. Plans should be made according to each child's needs and according to the guiding principles of minimizing loss and change. Parents who feel they would benefit from further input before they attempt to write the plan may wish to review the books recommended for parents in the List of References.

✔ 1. LEGAL CUSTODY

There are three legal custody options:

Joint Custody. Important decisions for the child are made jointly by the parents. Either parent may secure medical care, choose a school, or designate religious training, but parents should agree on what is best in these areas. Residence and parenting time schedules are separate.

Sole Custody. One parent has major decision-making responsibility in important areas including health, education, and religion. Residence and parenting-time schedules are assigned separately, as they are in joint custody.

Split Custody. One child (or more) is in the sole custody of one parent and the other child is in custody of the other parent. Separate parenting time schedules are necessary so that children may spend time with each other, as well as with each parent.

If both parents can make it work, joint legal custody is usually the best option. With joint custody parents should make every effort to consult each other about all important matters that affect the child. A decision for joint custody does not necessarily mean that the child will live in both homes.

When parents successfully exercise joint custody, the child's sense of family identity is maintained, and self-esteem is enhanced. The message is given throughout childhood that *both* parents are legally in charge. Even though parenting time may not be equal, children in joint custody families always know they can rely on both parents.

Joint custody will not be successful when one divorcing parent is abusive or when parents are in constant high conflict. When parents cannot agree on even minor aspects of daily life, at least one of them probably has not truly learned to put the needs of the child first. One or both parents may be insufficiently recovered from the spousal divorce and may still be unable to see that the child will benefit from having both parents as custodians.

In these situations, sole custody should be assigned to the parent most able to be flexible, to see that the child needs contact with the other parent, and to relate to the child most effectively. Split custody—designating separate custodians for separate children—should be considered only when the needs of each child clearly dictate that this would be best. (see Step 11)

If agreement cannot be reached on legal custody, co-parents should defer the decision temporarily, and proceed through the remainder of the Checklist. Eventually, an evaluator or the court may need to assist with this decision.

> You have to love your children unselfishly. That's hard. But it's the only way.
>
> Barbara Bush

✔ 2. RESIDENTIAL OR PHYSICAL CUSTODY

The child's residence is the home where he or she lives most of the time. The word "custody" is added to clarify which parent will handle the routine needs of the child. Primary residential assignments are commonly based on caretaking prior to separation. The parent who provided most of the routine care becomes the primary residential parent and will continue to have the majority of parenting time.

Joint legal custody with residential custody to one parent is currently a popular choice of custodial determinations. Children are emotionally secure when parents have decided to share legal decision-making but to assign a primary home. They rely on one parent more than the other for day-to-day care but know they have two parents who are legally responsible for them.

✔ 3. PARENT TIME-SHARE ROUTINE

Time with each parent should be maximized, even if a sole legal custodian or primary residential custodian is assigned. The exact schedule will be different for every family—personalities and wishes of both parents as well as those of the children should be considered.

Read Steps 10 and 11 before you decide parenting time schedules. Parents may find it convenient to refer to the prescribed patterns while writing their co-parenting plans. **However, these lists of patterns are only best guesses—general rules-of-thumb for children of different age levels. The recommendations are not laws that apply in every case. They should not be used as weapons or tools by poor co-parents looking for ways to exclude one another from the life of the child.**

Try to remember each parent's strengths and the children's needs when you set up routines. Include specific pick-up and drop-off times even if you are choosing joint custody and get along well. Most parents find that thorough discussions about the parenting time schedule are necessary, and adding specificity to your decisions will help.

✔ **4. HOLIDAYS AND BIRTHDAYS**

Major holidays are best split or shared between parents, whether there is joint, sole, or split legal custody. There are many ways to divide holiday time. One successful method is to make two lists of special days and assign each parent a set, then alternate the lists each year.

Family traditions become important to children as years go by, so it is best to discuss arrangements thoroughly as you write your co-parent plan. Specify which holidays are meaningful to you and be sure to include them on the list. You should consider discussing Christmas or Hannukah, New Years, Spring Break, Easter, Memorial Day, Independence Day, Labor Day, Halloween, Thanksgiving, and possibly others. Most people feel that Mother's Day should be spent with Mother and Father's Day with Father.

Scheduling holidays can be difficult when they interfere with the routine parenting time schedule. Usually it is best if holidays are given priority—they should be set on the calendar first, with the regular schedule resuming after the holiday. Co-parents do best if they maintain flexibility and work together to be sure the child does not go long periods of time without seeing one or the other of them. But parents should avoid inconvenient "make-ups" to balance missed time because of holidays. As with routine time-sharing, pick-up and drop-off times should be included.

Though parents often want to alternate spending the child's birthday with their son or daughter, disruptions can result when special days fall on school days. You may wish to consider letting the child's birthday be spent as it falls on the calendar instead, and ask the other parent to celebrate as near the date as possible. This arrangement allows the child's routine to be maintained, and it gives your son or daughter a second celebration to anticipate. No schedule changes should be made for parents' own birthdays—you each can celebrate whenever you are with your child.

✔ **5. VACATIONS**

Periodic vacations with each parent are beneficial to the child. Trips allow more relaxed interaction and often make it possible for children to see members of each parent's extended family. Vacations should not be too long for the child's developmental level, however, and they should not occur too often. Telephone calls to the other parent are important whenever children are away from home.

Because of the infrequency of vacations, guidelines for their duration may be more lenient than for routine time-share patterns. The following general rules, also included with the prescriptions for parenting time in Step 10, can be applied:

Infants — Birth to Two years

Vacations may be taken with the primary parent provided they do not separate the child from a highly involved secondary parent too long, for example, more than a week or so. Vacations with the non-primary parent are not recommended. Infants should not be separated overnight from the primary caretaker. As the child nears two years of age, one or two-night trips with the non-primary parent may be considered.

Toddlers — Two to Four years

Vacations with the primary parent are advisable if they do not create long separations from a highly involved non-primary parent. Children who have contact with the non-residential parent several times each week should not be separated from that parent more than a week or so. As children near three years of age, half-week vacations may be taken with a non-primary parent who has been routinely involved.

Pre-schoolers — Four to Six years

Vacations with the primary parent should not separate the child from an involved secondary parent more than ten days to two weeks. When the child is five years old, periodic week-long vacations can be considered for the non-primary parent unless he or she has not been routinely involved. When pre-schoolers do not see a parent regularly, trips or vacations with the less involved parent should be shorter than one week.

Early School Age — Six to Nine years

Vacations with the primary parent may be longer, up to three weeks, unless the child is accustomed to spending time with the other parent on a near half-time basis. When contact with both parents is frequent and nearly equal, vacations should be limited to two weeks. As children approach seven years of age, non-primary parents who have regular but shorter blocks of time may consider periodic two-week vacations as well. Children of early school age at the time of the divorce should experience shorter vacations before longer ones.

Pre-Adolescents — Nine to Twelve years

Vacations with the primary parent should not exceed three weeks if the time away will disrupt regular contact with the other parent. Non-primary parents who see their children often may plan two to three week vacations as the child nears ten years of age. Most children under twelve, however, still do best with trips limited to ten days to two weeks.

Adolescents — Twelve to Eighteen Years

Vacations with either parent may be longer than three weeks for children who are well-adjusted and have experienced gradually increasing separations from either parent. Shorter vacations are preferable when there are adjustment difficulties or when teens express hesitation at being gone from home too long.

✔ 6. DAYCARE

Most parents with young children find it necessary to have out-side help in caring for their children. First, it is best for parents to provide as much day-to-day child care as possible themselves. Each of you should take over for your co-parent when you can. When one of you has the day off from work, for instance, or even part of a day, you may arrange to share the child care that day. When working together is not feasible because your schedules coincide too closely, because there are long distances between your homes, or there is too much conflict between you, it is best to involve other caretakers. Try to share the burden of finding responsible adults on whom you both can rely and designate how the cost will be handled.

✔ **7. TRANSPORTATION**

Co-parents should share the chore of transporting their children from home to home. Helping each other in this way allows you to demonstrate support of one another. It is especially helpful when the parent with the greater amount of parenting time delivers the child to the secondary home. Your child senses encouragement and receives your permission to enjoy the company of his or her other parent. Delivering the child also eases the transition between homes, because the parent releasing the youngster can best prepare the child for the change.

✔ **8. POLICY FOR REARRANGING PARENTING TIME**

Parents should anticipate that changes in the routine time-share pattern will be necessary from time to time. But frequent changes are not good for the child—they are disruptive and make life unpredictable. **Especially in the first year after divorce, the schedule should be followed as strictly as possible.**

Co-parents need a plan for dealing with changes that *must* be made after the calendar for parenting time has been set. One method that works is to require the parent requesting a change to make it at least two weeks in advance.

The general rules to apply when schedules need to be temporarily rearranged are that keeping a consistent pattern is better, especially for younger children, and that children should not go long periods of time without seeing either parent. Often briefer periods of parenting time can be accomplished when a change has been requested. When children are ill, the time should be made up as promptly as possible. Arrangements for making changes like these should be constructed on a family-by-family basis.

✔ 9. MEDICAL DECISIONS

The legal custodian most often has responsibility for arranging the routine and major medical care of the child, unless parents decide or agree otherwise. When there is joint custody, *either* parent can secure treatment, but co-parents should be in agreement on the type of care and on who will be the providers. In sole custody families, non-custodial parents do not choose doctors, dentists, or therapists, but in most cases they may consult with the specialists who treat the children. Of course laws permit that either parent may secure emergency medical care during his or her parenting time, irrespective of legal custody.

✔ 10. SCHOOL DECISIONS

The legal custodian maintains the responsibility for choosing the child's school unless both parents agree otherwise or when joint custody has been selected. However, either parent may consult with teachers regardless of the assignment of custody. Fewer communication problems develop when each parent arranges to get information about the child's progress directly from the school. Co-parents should strive for a relationship harmonious enough for both to attend the child's school activities—though they need not necessarily sit together in the audience. Events at school are important to all children, and your child will be happy just to have both parents present.

Someday perhaps change will occur when times are ready for it, instead of always when it is too late. Someday change will be accepted as life itself.

Shirley MacLaine

✔ **11. RELIGIOUS UPBRINGING**

Like decisions about medical care and schooling, religious training is usually determined by the legal custodian. Parents settling on joint custody will come to a mutual decision about the child's spiritual involvement, but the child will not necessarily attend church or synagogue with both of them. Many separating couples find it best to delegate this responsibility to the parent who feels strongest about religion.

✔ **12. CHILD SUPPORT**

Every state has guidelines determining child support according to each parent's income. These guidelines will usually be applied unless you make other financial arrangements yourselves. Co-parents may choose to have their attorneys compute figures using the guidelines first and then work with each other to make further adjustments they feel will benefit the children. You should plan to review financial matters periodically and consider mediation if you have serious disagreements.

Compliance with the payment of child support is critical to your child's welfare. Parents who have persistent difficulties in collecting support as ordered by the court should pursue the matter through legal avenues. Cooperative parenting stops short of passive acceptance of this type of irresponsibility.

✔ **13. MEDICAL COSTS**

The co-parent with the best plan covering the children usually supplies the insurance. Co-pays and costs for medical, dental, and counseling needs that are not covered by insurance should be split or shared between the parents, equally or proportionately, according to income. It is advisable to reconcile medical expenses with each other on a timely basis, for example, monthly. This way neither parent is greatly inconvenienced and there will be less potential for conflict over these inevitable necessities.

✔ 14. COMMUNITY ACTIVITIES

Children are usually happiest taking part in sports and activities in the neighborhood of their *primary* residence.

> I know of no more encouraging fact than the unquestionable ability of man to elevate his life by conscious endeavor.
> Henry David Thoreau

Though this practice may be harder on the non-primary parent—who must travel or have parenting time disrupted—it is best for the child to maintain peer and community continuity. But primary parents also should take care not to schedule undue numbers of activities on the other parent's time. A general rule might be that no more than one ongoing activity at a time (e.g. scouts, baseball) should overlap the non-primary parent's time, and even these activities should be agreed upon.

✔ 15. TELEPHONE CALLS

It is best for children to have free telephone access to either parent, so long as calls are made at reasonable hours and there are no prohibitive, long-distance charges. Parents should voluntarily limit their *own* calls to children spending time in the other home, however, except when there are important reasons to call. When your child does not hear from you for some time, he or she feels free to relax in the other parent's care and enjoys parenting time more. You might consider calling your children under ten on a twice-weekly basis, and older children weekly. Calls to pre-school children should be only several minutes long under normal circumstances, but calls to children older than six usually may last longer, ten to fifteen minutes.

✔ **16. SHOPPING FOR CLOTHING**

It is usually best for the primary parent to do most of the shopping for clothing. A rule like this eliminates confusion for the child, as well as for both parents. You might decide to have the non-primary parent purchase designated items such as winter coats or shoes—and of course, gifts—on a regular basis.

✔ **17. ITEMS TO BE DUPLICATED**

Providing two complete sets of the most critical items at each home will make life go more smoothly. Most obviously, each child needs a bed and dresser or chest for clothing. Toys and grooming articles also should be duplicated if possible. Taking this step will cut down on inconvenience for both of you when important things are forgotten or become lost in the process of changing homes. Careful planning about the child's needs will minimize stress for everyone.

✔ **18. ITEMS TO BE SHARED**

Your child should be allowed to carry favorite possessions, including clothing, back and forth. Encouraging your son or daughter to take things along helps make transition easier and creates a way to "bridge" the homes. Parents should be conscientious about returning items the other parent may need to properly care for the child, such as eyeglasses, medicines, sports equipment, and uniforms. Special attention should be given to seeing that homework and school papers are returned. **This responsibility belongs to the parents throughout the early and middle school years. Children under ten or eleven will always need your help in making changes from home to home.**

✔ **19. INFORMATION TO BE EXCHANGED BETWEEN PARENTS**

Co-parents should always exchange their own addresses, telephone numbers, and vacation itineraries. Each parent should be available to the other in case of an emergency that involves the child. Former spouses should respect each other's privacy, however, and never intrude unnecessarily.

✔ **20. GRANDPARENT VISITS**

Grandparent relationships are important to the child and should be given consideration. It may be best for you to include time for them on a schedule most similar to what your child experienced before separation. Grandparent time may overlap each co-parent's time, or it may need to be included separately.

✔ **21. INVOLVEMENT WITH OTHER ADULTS**

Although newly separated spouses sometimes meet new partners quickly, it is best not to involve these adults with your children too soon, especially before the divorce is final. Even then, children should be introduced to parents' friends or dating partners gradually. Children should not be encouraged to form bonds or close relationships unless the new adults will have some permanence in the re-structured family. Unnecessary feelings of loss will be prevented in the event these relationships are only temporary.

When parents are seriously involved with new partners at the time they write their parenting plan, they should discuss how much contact with their boyfriends or girlfriends will make the children comfortable. Even if there will be a remarriage right away, step-parents should remain relatively detached. The child needs time to adjust to the new, restructured life and will do best if his or her nat-

---

There is nothing permanent except change.

Heraclitus

86

ural parents are still primary. Over time, step-parent relationships will be accepted by the child.

✔ 22. HOW CHANGES IN ROUTINE TIME-SHARE WILL BE MADE

Parenting time schedules that work at the time of separation will not suit the child over all the years to come. You should expect to re-think the time-share needs of your children periodically. Routines of small children usually need to be revised frequently to provide more time with non-primary parents as they grow older. Schedules of adolescents sometimes must be changed dramatically—these children have ideas and social needs of their own that must be taken into account. Some teens begin to resist the two-home concept even when they have changed homes frequently for some time. Others decide, rather abruptly, that they are now ready for equal time-sharing. A general guideline is that co-parents should plan to discuss parenting time patterns at least twice yearly while children are under seven years and annually when they are older.

✔ 23. CONSISTENCY BETWEEN HOUSEHOLDS

Neither parent should tell the other how to care for the child, but a general understanding of household consistency will help. It is best for parents to impose the same bed times, curfews, and overall style of discipline. One important rule should be that children sleep in their own beds in both homes, never with the parents. **Children often express their insecurities by asking, or demanding, to sleep with their mother or father.** But children who routinely sleep with parents develop emotional problems by becoming overly dependent. Parents should counter these requests and encourage children of all ages to sleep in their own beds.

✔ **24. SUPPORTING THE OTHER PARENT**

Parents should *always* encourage the relationship between the child and the other parent. There are many ways to support your co-parent, such as having the child ready to go on time, helping the child pack, and helping the child remember what to take to the other home. **Never undermine the other parent by being unprepared, by arriving unnecessarily early or late, or by threatening to send your child to the other home as "punishment."** Talk only in neutral or positive terms about your co-parent and tell your child that you are *both* capable of caring for him or her.

✔ **25. COMMUNICATING WITH THE OTHER PARENT**

Co-parents should provide each other directly with schedules, activity calendars, and notices of school events. Avoid asking the child to do your job by delivering messages or money to the other parent. If you cannot talk to each other without feeling conflict, write notes and send them by mail. Some parents find success using a parenting journal that they pass back and forth when the child changes homes. Entries—only about the children—keep each other informed and minimize the need to talk directly. You should use fax machines and telephone answering machines only with care: these devices do not assure confidentiality and therefore they do not entirely protect your child.

✔ **26. CONTROLLING CONFLICT**

Parents should commit themselves to controlling arguments in front of their children. Some may need to meet with each other only in the presence of a neutral, third person or in a neutral public place to prevent destructive eruptions of anger. Call co-parent meetings to address problems as they arise.

✔ 27. PROVISIONS FOR MEDIATION

Plan to use a mediator whenever you seriously disagree on major issues of parental concern—including discipline, child support, and division of parenting time. Be sure to include this provision in your finalized parenting plan. When co-parent meetings are not enough, taking this step will be the easiest route to problem resolution.

✔ 28. GEOGRAPHICAL MOVES

It is best for your child if parents reside within driving distance of each other. Long distance shared parenting is possible, but special time-share arrangements must be made in order to minimize loss of one parent. Often there will be more than the typically recommended amount of overnight time-sharing for younger children. The need for contact with the parent living far away will take priority over the need to make gradual increases in parenting time. Telephone calls also become more important; they may be longer, or more often.

When young lips have drunk deep of the bitter waters of Hate, Suspicion and Despair, all the love in the world will not take away that knowledge.

Rudyard Kipling

When children have had frequent contact with both parents for a long period of time, the decision to move should be made with great care. Your child will suffer a great loss when one of you moves away. Sometimes these decisions are made for the convenience of one parent, but they are generally not in the child's best interest.

✔ 29. PROVISIONS FOR HIGHER EDUCATION

Most people acknowledge the need for young adults to obtain some type of education beyond high school. It is best to discuss plans for your child's college or vocational schooling as early as possible, including plans for payment. Many parents set up special funds or bank accounts at the time of the divorce in order to anticipate this need.

COMPLETING THE AGREEMENT

After you have worked your way through the Checklist, you and your co-parent can take your worksheets to attorneys for preparation into legal form. If you wish, you can draft your own parenting plan, adapting the Sample Co-Parent Plan in Appendix B, and present this draft for finalization. The wording and tone of the Sample Agreement is based on a joint custody resolution, which is—and should be—the option chosen most frequently. If you select sole custody, the written style of your contract should still imply your intent for both of you to be involved and important.

In the event you have agreed on some, but not all, of the items on the Checklist, or if one partner has felt forced into false agreements, you may need assistance from a mediator or an attorney before you complete the plan. **Parents who have doubts about their tentative decisions should be sure to seek professional advice. Negotiations made in haste or under pressure will not yield a successful parenting plan.**

All current studies indicate that separation agreements left vague and non-specific add to the anxiety couples feel after divorce.

Divorcing spouses should write very complete plans or ask their attorneys to include all details they feel will help clarify what is expected of each of them after the separation is final. Proceeding in this way will give new co-parents the clearest, most business-like guidelines to follow, and it will help keep them out of conflict.

ADDRESS THE NEEDS OF THE CHILD WITH THE CO-PARENT CHECKLIST BEFORE COMPLETING THE PARENTING AGREEMENT

STEP 10 DETERMINING PARENTING TIME PATTERNS

Misconceptions abound among divorcing parents about how much input children should have in setting up the home-to-home schedule. The most common myth is that when a child reaches the age of 12 or 13, he or she will be able to choose the home or pick the parenting time pattern.

But there are good reasons why children should not determine their own time-share schedules any more than they should determine custody. These are serious adult issues to be decided between the parents according to what is best for each child. **When children do express preferences, either in words or in their behavior, caring co-parents will take these wishes into account, but they will not give the burden of absolute choice to a child of any age.**

No state has a law that gives absolute choice to a minor. Legislatures have determined that it would be harmful to assign such a large amount of responsibility to a child. Rather, courts follow a standard termed "best interests of the child" in assigning legal custody and parenting time. There are many criteria they consider in addition to the child's wishes, such as the quality of the parent-child relationships and the child's overall adjustment to the home, school, and community. Even when courts decide to give greater weight to voiced preferences of adolescents, they retain the right to rule otherwise when all factors are considered.

Often parents of even preschool children make the serious mistake of asking their sons and daughters outright which home they prefer, or whether the child wants more time with one parent than the other. In addition to misleading the child about his or her power, this type of questioning can set off feelings of alienation and cause the child to suffer excessive guilt about being unable to choose both.

Concerned co-parents of boys and girls at every age and developmental level should make decisions about parenting time together. Before the plan is completed, each parent should avoid telling the children about it prematurely. Then, after devising the plan, parents should present their choices to the children as their mutual decisions.

PRESCRIPTIONS BY AGE AND DEVELOPMENTAL LEVEL

Most parents know that specific patterns of parenting time are important to the child's welfare. In fact, these schedules are so important that child specialists now recommend general rules to be used when arranging them.

The following guidelines for time-sharing should be applied generally to children in normally adjusting families where there is only an average amount of conflict and stress. When there is a serious lack of cooperation, however, or when chronic abuse or violence occurs, parents will need to obtain professional guidance. Parents who are in constant high conflict need to follow more stringent schedules, and these should usually be designed with outside help.

It is important for mothers and fathers who do implement their own plans to understand that guidelines for dividing time are not intended to restrict the access of any loving parent to his or her child. They are meant to help you take into account the developmental needs of your individual children so you can set up a low-risk schedule. They also provide a recommended course of action when problems arise at each level.

Infants — Birth to Two Years

Children from birth to two years need consistency and routine in caretaking. They do best with a single, primary parent who is never gone from their environment more than several hours. For this reason, time with the other parent usually should not include overnight stays until the child is older. Frequent, shorter blocks of parenting time should be arranged if the non-primary parent is available.

When there is an older child in the family, the prescribed pattern may sometimes be changed to include overnights with the non-primary parent. The infant's attachment to his or her sibling will minimize the sense of losing the central caretaker, because the older child is almost always present in the world of the younger child. Co-parents should be cautious in taking this step, however. Children under age two quickly sense abandonment. They may have trouble establishing trust in others if the schedule calls for too much time away from the primary parent.

> I wept, and nothing happened, you did not come.
> Sarah Ferguson, writer

Infants and young children who are separated from the primary caretaker too long run the risk of being permanently distrustful and insecure. If the routine jeopardizes the child's stability there may be immediate symptoms of poor adjustment, such as crying, fussiness, and problems with eating or sleeping. At other times, symptoms may be delayed, for instance when an infant slowly becomes more withdrawn or grows more clingy over time.

Whenever distress signals of either type occur, parents should shorten the infant's contacts with the parent who is not primary, provided that taking this step will create more time with the primary parent rather than other caretakers. Later, when the troubling symptoms have disappeared, time with the secondary parent can be increased again.

- **Suggested Routine:** Establish one primary residence. Short, frequent stays of 1 - 4 hours with non-primary parent several times per week, increasing to 8 hours. No overnights at secondary home, unless in the company of an older child. Vacations with non-primary parent not recommended until child nears two years of age, when one or two night vacations may be considered.

- **Problem Indicators:** Excessive crying in the care of either parent, withdrawal or unresponsiveness, eating or sleeping difficulties.

- **Corrective Steps:** Shorten daytime contacts with secondary parent if this means contact with primary parent will be increased. Make environment calm and consistent.

Toddlers — Two to Four Years

Children aged two through four years still need consistent caretaking, but they begin to develop long-term memory and the ability to use language. Toddlers can spend longer periods of time with the parent who is not primary, including overnights, as they near three years of age. By now children are able to remember the missing parent for 24 hours or so. They still should return to the designated home-base before long, though, so the image of the primary caretaker can be refreshed.

Youngsters who are still mastering the steps of walking and talking may show the same signs of distress as infants when they are separated from the primary parent too long. Other symptoms may also develop because of their increasing awareness. Problem indicators in toddlers pointing to separation anxiety are clinginess, fear of abandonment, or demanding behavior in the company of either parent. Regression to earlier developmental stages is common, with backslides in behaviors such as thumb-sucking, toilet training, and sleeping through the night. If these symptoms persist, co-parents should consider reducing the length of visits temporarily and possibly eliminating overnights for the time being. Again, blocks of parenting time can be lengthened when the child's problems have been resolved.

- **Suggested Routine:** Increase length of daytime stays with non-primary parent gradually. As child nears three years of age, begin overnights one per week, increasing to two non-consecutive nights weekly, if parent has been highly involved. Periodic, half-week vacations with non-primary parent may be considered after age three.

- **Problem Indicators:** Fears of abandonment, regression to earlier behaviors, fussiness, anger while in the care of either parent.

- **Corrective Steps:** If symptoms occur often or persist over a period of days, reduce length of stays temporarily, provided that time spent with the primary parent will be increased. Eliminate overnights temporarily.

Children aged four through six years can spend more time in each home, even approximating half-time with each parent, as long as certain precautions are taken. The parents should reside in the same or close-by neighborhoods, so the child experiences minimal disruption in daily routine. The weeks should be split in half, not alternated in full, and increases from single overnights should be made gradually. Every effort should be made to unify the child's world, minimizing loss and constant change.

Young children not yet in school are still prone to blaming themselves for divorce, and they are afraid of losing both parents. A pattern providing for frequent time-share blocks with each parent and no more than a few days away from either one is often a very good choice. This schedule reassures the child that both parents are still there and counters feelings of loss.

While arranging equal contact can often benefit the child, a plan that *forces* a balanced schedule will result in stress. Sometimes circumstances simply do not lend themselves to this type of shared parenting. When parents live in separate cities more than 15 miles apart but struggle to equalize parenting time, for example, the children can be hurt by the disruptions. Young children must learn to socialize with playmates and adapt to part-time preschool programs. They should not routinely miss these important developmental experiences because the distance between homes makes travel back and forth inconvenient.

Preschoolers responding poorly to the parenting time schedule may continue to show their distress with sadness, anger, or signs of

> *Sorrow concealed, like an oven stopp'd,*
> *doth burn the heart to cinders where it is.*
> William Shakespeare

separation anxiety such as nightmares. They also may begin to enter power struggles with their parents and may seem poorly adjusted in either the primary or secondary home. **Mothers and fathers should be careful not to blame each other's behavior for these problems.** But if symptoms at home, preschool, or daycare persist longer than several hours after changing homes, and if they do not lessen over a period of weeks, parents should reduce the length of stays with the non-primary parent and consider eliminating overnights temporarily.

- **Suggested Routine:** Blocks of time with non-primary parent may increase from one to three overnights weekly. Begin to group two overnights together for older children. Some pre-schoolers do well with equal time-sharing, but many are still unable to handle separations, and overnights are inappropriate for them. Frequent day-long visits may be more beneficial as often as they are possible. Periodic, week-long vacations with the non-primary parent may be considered after age five.

- **Problem Indicators:** Crying, sadness, anger, power struggles, withdrawal, regression, tantrums while in the care of either parent.

- **Corrective Steps:** If symptoms persist, cut back on length of stays temporarily. Reduce the number of overnights for the time being, or group them together so the child has fewer transitions.

Early School Age — Six to Nine Years

Children age six through nine years need time with each parent to develop their unique personalities and to continue being reassured they are loved. Many are able to accommodate equal or near-equal parenting time patterns. They may still express a wish to reunite the family, but spending time with each parent more firmly establishes the reality of two homes. School-age children are also becoming interested in friends, and outside activities are more important.

When school-age children are in distress linked to the parenting time schedule, they may show sadness, anger, or aggressive behavior. They may have problems with friendships and in school. Some develop physical problems such as headaches or upset stomachs, or worry about growing up. Parents who cannot find other reasons for these symptoms may consider temporarily assigning a primary residence, giving the majority of parenting time to the parent who did most of the caretaking before divorce. Later, blocking overnights to reduce the number of household transitions may help. When you have temporarily discontinued overnights you may work back into them gradually.

> It is not a bad thing that children should occasionally, and politely, put parents in their place.
>
> Colette

- **Suggested Routine:** Equal time-share or near equal time-share works for many children. Weeks are best split in half, grouping the overnights together. Alternating weekends with mid-week daytime visits is still best for other children. Some children handle mid-week overnights well, but others find them disruptive. Two-week vacations with the non-primary parent may be considered after age seven, but only if week-long vacations have been taken first.

- **Problem Indicators:** Depression, anger, aggression, physical symptoms, decrease in friendships, school problems, fear of the future, fear of losing both parents.

- **Corrective Steps:** Temporarily assign a primary residence according to which parent did most of the caretaking before separation. Group overnights or reduce time-share with secondary parent so that time in primary residence is increased. Gradually work back into more overnights.

Pre-Adolescents — Nine to Twelve Years

Children aged nine through twelve years are becoming much more involved with their lives apart from their parents. When co-parents reside close to one another, equal time-sharing may work. But some pre-teens need different schedules to accommodate their changing priorities.

School and community needs begin to take precedence for children in this age group, and interest in peers continues to grow. School-age children may simply refuse to share time with parents equally, or even near equally, because of their competing interests. Although they have loving feelings for both parents, pre-teens' specialized needs are more important.

Most serious problems in the pre-adolescent years are related to depression and loneliness. Children who have few outlets for their emotions don't know what to do and are easily caught between their parents; they feel helpless about making things better. Children who *can* express themselves may become angry and oppositional, and increasingly blame their parents for divorce.

Pre-adolescents who do not adjust well often display school and learning difficulties. Many have problems with concentration, become hyperactive, and manifest reckless, thoughtless behavior. Some develop psychosomatic problems with accompanying physical symptoms. A particularly noticeable dynamic is one of "role-reversal," where the child attempts to care for a parent at his or her own emotional expense. A boy or girl who refuses invitations to be with friends because a parent may feel lonely, or who is fanatic about doing chores has lost the spark of youth. Co-parents should make efforts to remove these emotional burdens so their children's *own* needs may be better met.

> They mustn't know my despair, I can't let them see the wounds which they have caused, I couldn't bear their sympathy and their kind-hearted jokes, it would only make me want to scream all the more. If I talk, everyone thinks I'm showing off; when I'm silent they think I'm ridiculous; rude if I answer, sly if I get a good idea, lazy if I'm tired, selfish if I eat a mouthful more than I should, stupid, cowardly, crafty, etc. etc.
>
> Anne Frank

Separated parents addressing the problems of their pre-adolescents should first try blocking overnights with the non-primary parent, so as to cut down on transitions between homes. When problems are more serious, it is appropriate to increase time at the primary residence, even if overnights must be cut back, so the child will experience fewer disruptions and be able to concentrate on her or his own life. Again, these adjustments are usually temporary, and once the child is doing better parents can consider resuming the prior routine.

- **Suggested Routine:** Equal time with each parent benefits many children but is too disruptive for many. One primary residence with evenings and weekend time-share for non-primary parent is a pattern that often works. Mid-week overnights are successful for some children but not for others. Community and school activities must be maintained from both homes. Vacations longer than two weeks with the non-primary parent may be considered after age ten if child first has experienced a shorter vacation.

- **Problem Indicators:** Peer difficulties, loneliness, depression, anger, physical symptoms, learning problems, role reversals.
- **Corrective Steps:** Increase time at primary residence according to caretaking history prior to separation. Temporarily cut back on time-share with non-primary parent, especially overnights, if grouping them together first does not work.

Young Adolescents — Twelve to Fifteen Years

Adolescents aged twelve to fifteen years need the consistent support of both parents, but frequently they will not accept equal time-sharing. These children are beginning to individuate. They want to decide things for themselves, and they externalize blame to one or both parents. Young teens often become masters at parental manipulation—whether their parents are divorced or not.

When children in this age group do not adjust to divorce, many become more obstinate, act-out more frequently, or show poor performance in school. Some turn to drugs, alcohol, or sexual activity in an effort to deal with their anxiety. A few leave home or demand to switch residences constantly, as they try to control both parents. Parents may not recognize these behaviors as signs that their young teens need more stability and better parental cooperation, but behavior problems after separation are frequently signals of this kind of distress.

Mothers and fathers of early adolescents in serious emotional trouble should consult professional counselors who can help define the problems. Co-parents sometimes need to revert to a primary residential concept so the adolescent resides in a single home, either temporarily or permanently. In these cases it is usually best for the secondary parent to accept weekends or even just weekday hours with the child.

- **Suggested Routine:** Equal time-share is possible for some adolescents. Alternating weeks may work. Other teens need a primary residence with evenings and some weekends spent in the non-primary parent's home. Vacations up to one month with either parent may be considered if shorter vacations have been taken.

- **Problem Indicators:** Depression, moodiness, oppositionalism, acting out, poor school performance.

- **Corrective Steps:** Revert to a primary residential concept, temporarily or permanently. Time-share with secondary parent may be just weekends or even just weekday hours.

Older Adolescents — Fifteen to Eighteen Years

Older teens still need consistent support of their mothers and fathers, even though their peers have become more important. Many adolescents de-idealize one or both parents. A normal task of this age group is for teens to prepare for emancipation. By identifying inadequacies in their parents they naturally make leaving home easier.

When parents divorce, many older teens quickly become intolerant of parental problems. These adolescents are prone to *accelerated* emancipation—they may look for ways to leave home too soon, before they are able to handle responsibility. Many sense regression in their mothers and fathers, as they observe their parents dating or behaving like teens themselves. Others simply tire of worrying about their parents at a stage when their own needs for independence are prominent.

Parenting time patterns for older adolescents must often be the most flexible of all. First, it helps parents to understand that serious dissatisfactions are normal for this age group, and usually they do not reflect either parent's shortcomings. Mothers and fathers should try not to blame one another when maturing teens side with one parent against the other or reject a parenting schedule that includes time spent in both homes.

> You can exert no influence if you are not susceptible to influence.
>
> Carl Jung

When older adolescents act out by developing school failure or attendance problems, get into legal trouble, or run away from home, parents should take serious action to stabilize the residential arrangement. A primary home should be designated on a permanent basis for these children, and it is critical to avoid a power struggle with the youngster about choosing the home. Input from the teen should be considered paramount in deciding parenting time. Sometimes older adolescents must decide their own living arrangements entirely.

- **Suggested Routine:** Equal parent time-share is possible for some older adolescents. Others need a primary residence with day and weekend time in company of the other parent.

Some do best to see the non-primary parent regularly but only for several hours at a time. Vacations longer than one month may be considered.

- **Problem Indicators:** Acting out, oppositionalism, depression, poor school performance, leaving home, trouble with the law.
- **Corrective Steps:** Assign a primary residence on a permanent basis. Follow the child's wish on time-share and vacations.

TIME-SHARING DIFFICULTIES

Four common problems are identified by parents attempting to apply the prescriptions for dividing parenting time. These can be outlined briefly so that you may address them when they arise.

Unpredictable Work Schedules

When parents' work hours change on a weekly or half-weekly basis, it can be difficult or even impossible to find a regular parenting time pattern. In these cases the primary residence concept becomes more important. Because children do not adapt to change easily, they do not do well when household shifting is irregular.

Parents with changing work patterns will need to set up less definite parenting time schedules built around certain consistencies. For instance, it might be agreed that the parent who is not primary will always see the child twice per week and have one overnight stay, but the dates will need to be determined at the start of each work week. Because of disruptions caused by fluctuating arrangements, often it is best when children have fewer total overnights outside the primary residence.

Long Distance Time-Sharing

Time sharing is difficult to arrange when parents live far apart from each other. Distances that require driving longer than one-half hour make transfers stressful if they occur several times per week. Trips that take several hours are even more taxing and are usually too disruptive to occur frequently. Children who are forced to travel long distances too often usually develop symptoms of poor adjustment; parents should be aware of this possibility from the outset.

Several guidelines can be helpful to co-parents setting up long distance parenting time patterns, for example, when parents reside in different states:

• Assign a primary residence. It is rarely feasible for children to share homes on an equal or nearly equal basis when the parents reside long distances apart.

• Assign parenting time with the out-of-state parent on a periodic basis so that trips are not required too often. Most children can handle inter-state trips scheduled several times per year, but few can handle them as often as monthly.

• When the child is in the care of the non-primary parent, apply the general prescriptions for time-sharing on a liberal basis. Exceptions to standard recommendations, for example allowing more overnight stays at a younger age, can be made in the interest of prioritizing the importance of seeing the other parent. **So long as deviations from the usual guidelines are neither drastic nor too frequent, the overall benefit of making parent contact possible will outweigh the risk of longer separations from the primary parent.**

Once children have started school, of course, their need for consistency in the academic routine must also be balanced against their need to see both parents.

• Share the burden of travel. For younger children especially, parents can usually arrange more periods of contact per year by taking turns traveling to each other's community. Many are able to stay with relatives or friends in the vicinity of the other parent for several days or even a week or more and arrange day visits or overnight stays with the non-primary parent. Some parents even secure hotel or motel lodging for this purpose.

• Consider unescorted airline travel for children over age 8, making certain all precautions are taken and airline regulations for child travel are adhered to.

Again, parents should not push children to adapt to constant travel, unreasonably long periods of time away from home, or constant separations from the primary parent at any age level. A child of even teenage years who has never experience parental separation may be faced with considerable anxiety if co-parents construct an inappropriate time-share pattern.

Transition Adjustment Reactions

Transition refers to the period of time the child is adjusting to being with one parent or the other. The adjustment begins in the home the child is leaving and ends after the child has settled down in the other home. Parents report more difficulties with this adaptation than any other aspect of time-sharing.

Transitions are naturally difficult for children of any age. Whenever boys or girls change home environments they are reminded of the loss caused by divorce, and they tend to react strongly. But the ease of changing homes also may be related to the time-sharing pattern or to the behavior and feelings of *parents*. If you are sensitive to the stress that is expected whenever the child leaves one parent to go to the other, you will be able to make things go more smoothly.

Parents should take care not to blame each other for normal symptoms of adjustment difficulty. In young children there frequently is crying, clinging, anger, and oppositional behavior in either home near the time of the transfer. Older children may show avoidance, dawdle, or refuse to get ready to go. **Often the stress of transition is vented in negative or unruly behavior in the home the child is returning to. Concerned parents should look for other sources of stress before they conclude either parent is mishandling the situation.**

> Once you bring life into the world, you must protect it. We must protect it by changing the world.
> Elie Wiesel

Though problems of transition are normal, parents often ask how long symptoms should last. Each child's response will vary, just like other aspects of his or her adjustment. Younger children and older children with difficult inborn temperaments are most at risk for having these kinds of problems.

To address issues of transition responsibly, parents should consider that a child may need a block of parenting time lengthened to settle in the secondary home more comfortably. Another child, in contrast, may need to have a scheduled contact shortened or eliminated instead. For example, sometimes an overnight change of homes in mid-week becomes too disruptive for the child. The schedule may need to be cut back to allow only an evening block of time. **Parents should always try changing the pattern slightly before eliminating parental contact altogether.**

• The parent **releasing** the child should calmly prepare the
child to go. Always take time to get the child ready, emotionally and physically. Talk about the upcoming transition and
help the child pack things to take. Always be positive about
the other parent and the other home.

• The parent **receiving** the child should let the child adjust
slowly. Do not have busy plans at the start of a block of parenting time. Spend the first hours calmly, preferably at home,
sitting and talking with the child. If visits are short, spend
the entire time at home or in the same place every time.

Problems of transition are further addressed in Step 12, which
focuses on how parents use time with the children. Mothers and
fathers who *think through* the difficulties of changing homes from
the child's point of view are best able to structure parenting time
and minimize disruption.

Time-Share Refusals

Children under three years may show resistance to changing
homes by prolonging their clingy or angry behavior at times of transition. Children over age three may become even more obstinate
and clearly refuse to go. School-age and adolescent children can
become blatantly unwilling to comply with their parents' decisions.

Parents should first deal with refusals for time-sharing by
reviewing the current routine together, making certain the child is

not being required to exercise a grossly inappropriate pattern. You should make corrections according to the suggestions in the guide-lines when you need to. In addition, you should attempt to identify other factors that might be affecting your child's unwillingness to cooperate. Mothers and fathers have great influence over their children's attitudes toward the other parent. Encouragement and positive preparation will always help, while discouragement in the form of criticism or alienation of the other parent will make matters worse.

Children who refuse to participate in time-sharing in spite of the non-primary parent's desire to see the child are usually responding to heightened conflict between the adults. Either parent's anxiety or disapproval of the other is projected onto the child, and resistance to time-sharing will continue until you address the conflict yourselves.

As with your other negotiations, you should strive to maintain a business orientation when you apply the parenting time prescriptions. You should demonstrate acceptance of the fact that your child's needs must come first, even if that means your own time with the child may have to be decreased so your son or dauthter can cope with life more easily. When children develop serious problems going from home to home, their symptoms communicate to parents a need for some kind of change.

THE CHILD'S AGE, DEVELOPMENTAL LEVEL, AND ADJUSTMENT AFFECT THE PARENTING TIME PATTERN

STEP 11 CUSTOMIZING THE CO-PARENT PLAN

Every child is an individual with specific needs and interests. Parents who have more than one child should think about their children separately as well as together. At times this will mean making separate decisions, such as allotting one child more blocks of time with the non-residential parent than another. It also takes more co-parent work to assure that the needs of each child are met.

Brothers and sisters with customized parenting plans may well have different routines. The schedules should take into account the children's needs to be with *each other* as well as the need to be with each parent.

Three hypothetical examples will illustrate some possibilities:

Example 1

A child needs extra time with the same-gender parent

Jennifer, age 12

Nick, age 10

In this family, Mother was the primary caretaker before separation. She was at home more of the time to take care of the children's day-to-day needs—fixing meals, doing laundry, helping with school work. Now the parents are divorcing, and they decide it will be best if Mom continues as primary residential parent. The basic pattern they choose is to alternate Friday and Saturday nights with each parent while the children live with their mother during the week.

Nick, however, is developing more interest in sports and is expressing a wish to spend extra time with his father. Both parents are sensitive to this need, and they want to arrange more time for Nick to be with Dad. They decide that Nick will benefit from spending every Thursday overnight with his father. Jennifer will have individual time with her father on Wednesdays after school, but she will not stay overnight. Both parents feel Jennifer needs to be back with her mother on school nights.

Routine:
Nick will be with Mom Sunday through Wednesday nights and alternating weekends. He will be with Dad every Thursday night and the other weekends.

Jennifer will be with Mom Sunday through Thursday nights and alternating weekends. She will be with Dad every Wednesday, 4 to 8 p.m. and the other weekends.

Example 2

Children need very different schedules
Jack, Age 6
Scott, Age 1

In this family with two boys, the parents make other customized arrangements. First, they recognize that their older son has an exceptionally strong bond with his father even though he also is close to his mother. Jack's primary attachment seems to be with his father, and they arrange for near-equal parenting time but slightly more time with Dad than Mom.

Scott, however, is still in the infant stage of development. His mother has done most of his caretaking, and Scott needs the consistency of his mother's home. The parents live close to each other, so it is possible for Scott to be with his father frequently, usually while Jack is at Dad's home as well.

Jack and Scott will learn from the outset of their parent's separation that they are individuals as well as brothers. These children are five years apart in age. Their pattern of time-sharing might always differ somewhat, even though both parents acknowledge that someday Scott may also need more time with Dad.

Routine:

Jack will be with Dad Sunday through Tuesday nights and alternating weekends. He will be with Mom Wednesday and Thursday nights and the other weekends.

Scott will be with Mom every overnight. He will be with Dad 5-8 p.m. every Monday, Tuesday, and Thursday and 12- 6 p.m. every other Saturday and Sunday. Jack is usually at Dad's when Scott is there, but on Thursdays Scott and Dad spend the evening hours together while Jack is at Mom's home.

Example 3

Children need separate residences

Haley, Age 18

Jamie, Age 14

In this hypothetical family the parents select the unusual arrangement of designating separate primary residences. Many factors lead to their decision to choose split residential custody for their daughters, and much thought goes into how the time-share will work.

Haley is a senior in high school, and Jamie is in the ninth grade. Father has decided to remain in the family home, but Mother will relocate to a neighboring community. Haley feels strongly about graduating with her current senior class, and therefore her parents allow her to choose to stay with Dad.

Jamie, in contrast, is just entering high school. It will be easier for her to make friends in a new neighborhood and to adjust to a new school. With Jamie's input, her parents decide that their younger daughter will live with Mom. But they arrange for the sisters to be together *every weekend*—alternating Friday and Saturday nights with each parent.

Routine:

Haley will be with Dad all week and will spend alternate Friday and Saturday overnights with Mom. Haley and Jamie will spend every weekend together. Haley will also be with Mom every other Sunday overnight, and Jamie will be with Dad for these nights.

Jamie will be with Mom all week and will spend alternate Friday and Saturday overnights with Dad. She will spend every weekend with Haley. Jamie will also spend every other Sunday night with Dad, when Haley is at Mom's.

Though it may seem surprising, the split-residence concept is sometimes the best choice for children. In addition to instances like the example above, it can be best to split up children of any age who have special problems. If siblings become violent with each other or with one parent, for example, they may do better if they live in different homes but get together on a planned schedule. **Parents should be aware that the decision to separate brothers and sisters can be traumatic, as it creates loss of a sibling as well as loss of a parent.** This option should be reserved only for special circumstances.

ONE-ON-ONE TIME

Whenever there is more than one child in a family, parents should try to arrange individual time for each child with each parent. Time alone provides for a unique kind of togetherness children love. During one-on-one time, parent and child can explore mutual interests and discover what they have in common. The child has the chance to experience his or her importance to the parent providing this very special attention.

In the case examples outlined, all six children were assigned weekly one-on-one time with the non-primary parent. There are many ways to arrange private parenting time in addition to these ideas. One pattern that works is to have the secondary parent rotate a three to four hour block of time with the children, one at a time, on a designated weekly afternoon or evening. Another way is to specify that one parent will always be in charge of taking a child to a routine activity or sport. This contact creates extra personal time, and it also makes an opportunity to support the child's participation in activities.

"Dad, how come Mom never has time for just me? I remember when we used to count all my stuffed animals and talk about when I grow up—just the two of us."

A nine year old girl asking for one-on-one time with her mother.

OTHER CONSIDERATIONS

Arranging the best parenting time plan for each child often involves other complex issues. At times there are half-siblings or step-siblings in the family. Decisions must be made about splitting these children for visits and including time for other important adults. When long distances are involved between the communities, frequent home change is just not possible, even though it may be best for infants and small children.

It is outside the scope of this basic parenting guide to include advice for the myriad of possible post-divorce family constellations. A few simple guidelines will help co-parents—and even *networks* of parenting figures—come up with creative and workable schedules that are best for each individual child.

Parents Come First

Time with both original parents should be maximized. Contact with the non-residential parent should usually take priority over time with a step-parent, grandparent, day-care provider, or other adult involved in the child's life. **Step-parents, in particular, may be asked by the divorcing mother and father to step back and assume a more distant role, so they do not replace either parent of the child's nuclear family.**

Full-Sibling Relationships Come First

Relationships where all children share the same mother and father usually are more important than half-sibling relationships, where there is only one parent in common, or step-sibling relationships, where neither parent is shared. Visits and parenting time patterns should give priority to keeping full-siblings together, splitting them less frequently and for shorter periods of time.

Cut Back When There Are Signs of Distress

Simplify visitation and time-share situations that become chaotic and unworkable. Eliminate less critical commitments first and apply the rule on a child-by-child basis. This concept frequently will mean cutting back on activities for younger children and cutting back on time-sharing for older children, especially adolescents.

Parents should remember that the importance of day-to-day contact with both mother and father is greatest when children are small. It decreases in lieu of less frequent, but consistent, meaningful, contact as they mature. Older children and teens need to develop themselves as they relate to peers and the world they live in. For them, the role of both parents becomes primarily one of guidance and support.

> Each child is an adventure into a better life—an opportunity to change the old pattern and make it new.
>
> Hubert Humphrey

Parents who cooperate should meet on a regular basis to discuss the caretaking needs of their children. As stated in Step 7, you should meet at least twice yearly when your children are under age seven or so and at least annually when they are older. Changes that seem necessary should be enacted voluntarily whenever both parents see the need, and when you agree on how to improve the patterns of your involvement.

EACH CHILD SHOULD BE CONSIDERED INDIVIDUALLY

STEP 12 MAKING THE MOST OF PARENTING TIME

Once parenting time has been divided, each former spouse should make sure his or her style of caretaking benefits the child. Whether you are the primary or non-primary parent—whether you see your child often or only occasionally—the way you use your time with your child is very important.

First, parents should clearly outline the co-parent time-sharing plan to their children. You can use a calendar and colored markers to define for each child what his or her routine will be. Boys and girls even at age three are able to understand schedules presented to them in graphic form—it gives them something tangible to hold on to.

Older children and adolescents also do well to see the pattern outlined visually. For them, the point is to emphasize the importance of their time with you and with the other parent as well. In addition, providing a calendar helps them avoid—or at least anticipate—conflicts with activities and friends.

PARENTING ROLES

By far the majority of divorced parents look forward to spending time with their children, and few see parenting as a burden. The parenting problems that *do* arise often stem from former spouses' concerns about caretaking. Many mothers and fathers complain about not feeling able to provide for their children's needs in the short time they are allotted. Others complain—sometimes inappropriately—about the other's poor use of parenting time.

It will be helpful to break down your role as a parent into specific functions.

1. Parents Nurture Their Children. They feed, clothe, and care for them physically—when they are well and when they are ill. Nurturant parenting entails setting up safe, clean, stable surroundings and providing necessities children need to feel secure at all times.

2. Parents Guide Their Children. They provide a structure for life with rules, expectations, and good examples, so children know how to behave. Discipline and consequences are functions of guidance, but so are communication and understanding. Parents who guide their children with empathy nudge them gently toward healthy growth and development.

3. Parents Teach Their Children. By arranging a wide variety of experiences, parents impart their own knowledge and interest in the world to their sons and daughters. When adults read to children, help with schoolwork, and arrange outings, they expose their young to information and learning. They also model their own eagerness for involvement, so the child may internalize the value of personal growth.

4. Parents Enjoy Their Children. When mothers and fathers share in pure fun and excitement with their youngsters, they strengthen parent-child attachments and encourage healthy bonding. They impart a sense of approval for the child to feel good and happy. By sharing pleasant moments and experiences, parents give their children positive messages and memories of gratification.

If you are the parent with the greater amount of time with your children, you probably can identify each parental role as emerging naturally in daily life. If you are the parent with shorter or less frequent blocks of time, though, you may struggle to fit them in. But there are ways to fulfill all four parent functions in the time you are assigned, even if your parenting time is brief. By forming simple habits about structuring parenting time efficiently you will see it can be done.

QUALITY PARENTING TIME

Non-primary mothers and fathers have the task of finding briefer, less frequent ways of fulfilling the functions of a parent and the chore of juggling roles. Those parents who accept the reality of time constraints do better than those who try to force too many kinds of parenting into every block of time together—or those who repeatedly sacrifice one function to emphasize another.

> I looked on child rearing not only as a work of love and duty, but as a profession that was fully as interesting and challenging as any honorable profession in the world and one that demanded the best I could bring to it.
>
> Rose Kennedy

Parents with time-share blocks of only several hours can nurture, guide, teach, and enjoy their children, whenever they use the right approach. This is because it is the *quality* of interactions that makes the difference to the child—not the quantity. **Whenever parents choose quantity over quality they run the risk of adding stress for the child.**

Children who are constantly on the go when they are with the non-residential parent, for example, become worn out and tired. Primary parents describe symptoms of overload in boys and girls after hectic visits with driven, overactive non-primary parents. When schedules are crammed with special events, meals eaten out, and visits to extended family, children have trouble settling down and making transitions back to the primary home. Often they do not eat or sleep well, and frequently they are agitated as they return to school the next day.

At the other extreme are children who are neglected in one way or another during time with the non-primary parent. In some families boys and girls are consistently left in the care of step-parents, grandparents, or babysitters for large portions of the natural parent's time. Or a co-parent too anxious to enjoy the children will ignore needs to complete school and homework assignments, and overlook the roles of guidance and teaching. Self-indulgent habits like these defeat the real purpose of parenting time, which is to allow opportunity for you to exercise *all* your parent functions.

STRUCTURING PARENTING TIME

Parents in both the primary and non-primary positions can follow procedures that will help them make good use of their time. These steps allow for communication between adults and children—they also follow the principles of making small and gradual changes for transitions between homes. Most importantly, they provide a way for cooperative parents to be sure they attend to all parental role functions.

1. Begin Parenting Time with a Quiet Family Meeting. Sit and talk with your children in the car or your home for at least thirty minutes. Avoid proceeding straight to activities or introducing too much stimulation too early in your block of time. Your child needs the opportunity to adjust to being with you and re-orient his or her thinking to your plans.

When you talk as a family for even fifteen minutes, you can nurture, guide, teach and enjoy your child.

2. Get Input About the Child's Needs. Ask your children how they feel, whether they are tired or hungry. Avoid interrogation about the other parent, because questions like these will make the transition period difficult. Show more interest in your child than you do in yourself or your own plans and ideas. Although you already may have communicated with your co-parent about what the child needs, find out from the child directly what you might have to do to make him or her feel attended to.

3. Set a Schedule for the Block of Time. First, make a schedule for necessities, like meals, naps, homework, or practicing a musical instrument. If your time together is short, avoid overemphasis on chores and duties. These will interfere with your other parental functions.

Once necessities are scheduled, fit in educational or pleasurable activities as best you can. When blocks of time are short, you may only be able to play board games and read books with your child to exercise the roles of enjoyment and teaching. When parenting time blocks are longer you will be able to schedule more exciting outings.

Non-primary parents should bear in mind that children experience immense gratification from even small interactions with parents. When you take a moment to put a band-aid on your child's scraped knee or review your proud child's schoolwork, you seize the chance to parent well. You impart your love with emphasis and fulfill your parental responsibility in an instant.

4. Follow the Schedule with Flexibility. Remember that the plan is only a blueprint for your parenting time. Details may need to be altered as the hours or days progress. If your child is stuck on a homework assignment, for instance, your role as teacher must come first, and even the board game may have to wait until your next get-together.

5. End Parenting Time with a Review. This brief re-cap of what you have done will be a shorter family meeting than the one when you first received your child. A personal talk like this provides important closure to your time together, and it helps prepare for transition to the other parent's home.

Your review should include a discussion of the general plan for your next block of parenting time, and it should allow a moment for your child to express feelings. Taking time to finish your visit in this way solidifies your relationship by communicating unequivocally that your child is important to you.

LONG-DISTANCE PARENTING

When there are great geographical distances between non-primary parents and their children, there are fewer blocks of parenting time. Usually your visits provide *longer* periods of contact, however, and these can easily be structured for excellent parent-child interaction. **Parents residing far away from their children miss fre-**

quent contact, but they usually have deeply gratifying and meaningful visits when they are with their sons and daughters.

If you are a long-distance parent, you can take other steps to increase your parental involvement when you are not spending time with your child. In addition to making regularly scheduled phone calls, you can write letters back and forth, send tapes and videos of yourself—even mail magazine or newspaper clippings that you know will interest your child. These "bridges" let you nurture, guide, teach, and enjoy your child almost as often as you would like. Although living apart is difficult, there are ways to make it work, for yourself as well as for your child.

Parents who must share their children are encouraged to look at the "big picture" with regard to their parental roles. If you can get over your own losses and keep in mind that from the youngster's viewpoint, childhood is a long time, you will be able to accept the limitations for now, and make the most of your parenting efforts. Over the years to come there *will* be chances for quality interaction with your child, and many opportunities that will count.

THE QUALITY OF THE PARENT-CHILD RELATIONSHIP IS THE SUM TOTAL OF THE QUALITY OF ALL ITS PARTS

STEP 13 SOLVING COMMON PROBLEMS

Parents implementing their co-parenting plan often run into problems. More difficulties occur between parents than with children, probably because the burden of making the plan work is almost entirely on the adults. Even when there are problems that appear to be with children directly, the source is usually rooted in parental dynamics.

COMMUNICATION BREAKDOWNS

No matter how determined one or both parents may be to maintain courtesy and neutrality, lapses in communication occur with most divorced couples. Trouble signs include escalation of angry tones during talks, unreturned phone calls, or failures to trade information about the child until it is too late. **Never ignore communication barriers.**

The first parent to notice the breakdown should bring it to the attention of the other. A meeting may be necessary to iron out the problem face-to-face using negotiation techniques like those outlined in Step 7. When feelings are too negative for you to meet in person it is better to communicate in writing, sending messages by mail or personal hand delivery. If you have chronic difficulty talking to each other you can resort to a child-log or journal in which you trade information regularly, as your child changes homes.

Cooperative parents should never ask the child to take care of parental communication by discussing problems with former spouses for them. If you make the mistake of dragging the child into adult business, you raise the likelihood that your son or daughter will feel the negative effects of your avoidance. You create a destructive impasse to divorce recovery rooted in your own unresolved grief.

"I can't stand it. It hurts too much to see them go. I'm all torn up inside."
A grieving spouse.

EMOTIONAL TRANSFERS

Letting go of your children to give them to the other parent for a block of parenting time is often very difficult. Releasing the child sets off feelings of loss that plague every divorcing parent. Transferring the children—taking them to the other home or retrieving them yourself—can therefore be a troublesome time. Mothers and fathers often complain that the parent delivering a child arrives upset, and is abrupt, rude, or otherwise invasive of adult personal space. Many report that the parent giving up a son or daughter cannot separate from the child, displaying his or her own anxiety with anger or tears. There are two ways of transferring children that help:

- Transfer the children in a neutral place; for example at the public library.
- Transfer the children in the presence of a neutral person or agent; for example, the daycare provider or school.

It is important that parents recognize that the transfer itself creates problems. Difficulties must be addressed in ways that protect the children from conflict. You should work toward going back to transferring children directly from home-to-home as soon as you are able.

MONEY PROBLEMS

Divorcing spouses always experience financial difficulty. Experts compute it would take an additional one-third combined income in order for both households to be maintained without a setback. Both parting spouses usually feel the crunch. Often the primary parent needs more money from the other parent in order to care for the children, but the non-primary parent can have trouble supporting herself or himself once the child support is paid.

> Money, which represents the prose of life, and which is hardly spoken of in parlors without an apology, is, in its effects and laws, as beautiful as roses.
> Ralph Waldo Emerson

Mediators should be sought to address serious financial concerns that arise before and after the divorce. Rules may need to be included in the parenting plan to penalize a parent who is chronically delinquent with payment. In cases of extreme irresponsibility, parents should seek legal advice about collecting unpaid support.

Parenting time should never be cut back, withheld, discouraged, or bartered because of money. Neither should financial problems be shifted irresponsibly to the child, as in cases where an angry parent offers to pay child support directly to a teenage son or daughter rather than the ex-spouse. Co-parents should know they harm their children when they resort to common attempts to control one another with money.

DISAGREEMENTS ABOUT DISCIPLINE

Children often become difficult to handle when separation occurs, and parents can have problems with discipline they never had before. This is understandable, since children's lives are usually less stable than they were before divorce and the grieving process is painful. Boys and girls often react to situational anxiety and negative feelings with behavioral resistance.

Children can adapt to different expectations and different sets of household rules, provided the rules in both homes are clear. Although you should agree to use the same basic *style* of discipline if you can, you should not tell each other what to do. Criticizing your co-parent's decisions will undermine your support of his or her competence, and it will hurt your child.

Your child needs to learn to deal with both parents as individuals after divorce. Consequences for poor behavior should be home-specific, and not carried from house to house. **A child should never be sent to the other home when he or she has misbehaved.**

Methods of disciplining children in separate households are no different than methods of disciplining them in the same home. Of the three following types of discipline styles, only the third is recommended:

- **Authoritarian.** This extreme style of parenting is strict, rule-bound, and harsh. The parent expects and demands compliance without much input from the child. Punishment is excessive. The child may be disciplined physically or grounded for weeks. Even if adults in both homes agree about this style of discipline, serious problems will develop sooner or later, because the purpose of this kind of management is unreasonable control by the parent, and not healthy growth of the child.

- **Permissive.** The other extreme style is too loose, with few rules, expectations, or consequences. A parent feeling guilty

So long as little children are allowed to suffer, there is no true love in this world.
Isadora Duncan

about divorce may not be firm enough, and may be ruled by a child he or she is trying to please. Boys and girls handled this way become demanding and self-centered. Input from them is too important, and they become directors of their own lives. When children are over-indulged they become hard to live with, and noticeably unhappy. Parents trying to rectify the situation will find it difficult, because children given too much control in the first place always resist having it taken away.

• **Firm-but-Flexible.** The best child-rearing approach involves the parent as *authoritative* head-of-household, and as organizer of the child's expectations. In a family using this style of parenting, general rules are clear and easily followed by the child, but they may be changed with the child's input. Consequences involve loss of privileges, time-outs, or reasonable grounding. A child is never disciplined physically or sent to his or her room for excessive periods of time. Appropriate grounding, for example, would be approximately 15 minutes for children under five years, 30 minutes for children five to ten years, and at most, one half-day for pre-teens and teens. There should always be built-in rewards for good behavior, and most important, unconditional love.

One reason firm-but-flexible parenting works best in families after divorce is that it is not extreme. After the general approach is agreed upon co-parents need not have concern for the other's style of discipline. It becomes easy for you to accept parenting decisions of your former spouse if you know discipline will not be too harsh or too permissive. Boys and girls themselves also accept two sets of household rules most readily if both are set up with firm flexibility.

WHEN CHILDREN COME BETWEEN PARENTS

Children manipulate parents by coming between them only when there is a *possibility* of pitting one against the other. At first it may be unconscious but over time they learn to complain about, reject, or lie about first one household, then the other. Youngsters do this because of the reactions they get and the attention they receive. Allowing your child to control you is dangerous to his or her well-being, however, for it encourages the development of a shrewd and devious personality.

Successful co-parents combat manipulation by maintaining their own coalition whenever the child tries to split them. They develop habits of calling each other and discussing the child's reports in a business-like way, or find other ways to check out data given by the child. If you believe only the negative reports that you yourself witness or check out thoroughly, you will head off most of the maneuvering.

A MISSING PARENT REAPPEARS

When one parent returns after leaving the child in the care of the other for a long period of time after separation, problems occur for both natural parents and for the child.

Parents should first recall the premise of Part I of this book, which suggests that there is value in re-introducing a missing parent who now plans to become involved. Except when a parent's legal rights have been terminated, the child will benefit from seeing a loving parent once again—even if the parents were never married. **So long as the mother or father is sincere about remaining involved and will not disappear again, the child's sense of identity will be strengthened through contact.**

Secondly, parents should follow the principles of *small* and *gradual change* when discussing parenting time for one who has not been in the child's life. Though the child's loss will be lessened by "finding" the missing parent, the introduction of too much contact too soon will be hard for the child to handle. In some instances visits with the missing parent are easiest at first if they actually include the child's primary parent or another familiar adult. Mediators or other professionals may be needed to advise parents in these cases.

STEP-FAMILY COMPLICATIONS

Until recently men and women who married parents with children have tried to fit the blended families into a nuclear family model. Their aim has been, in essence, to replace the stable networks they lost when one or both of them divorced. But repeatedly step-parents have reported frustration and disappointment as they encounter problems with overzealous attempts at family reconstruction.

Now we know the co-parenting relationship of the *original* family is critical to the child, and we can tell step-parents what to expect. One guideline is that the step-family structure will be looser than that of the original family. Step-parents will usually be less involved with step-children than they are with their own children. The model of "one happy family" simply does not apply. Step-parents assuming more distant roles similar to those of "aunts" or "uncles" often do best.

> Selective ignorance, a cornerstone of child rearing. You don't put kids under surveillance: it might frighten you. Parents should sit tall in the saddle and look upon their troops with a noble and benevolent and extremely nearsighted gaze.
>
> Garrison Keillor

135

Another updated expectation for step-families is that the person who marries one ex-spouse will have to tolerate the new partner's continuing involvement with the other ex-spouse. Co-parents are going to have talks and meetings throughout the coming years, and these contacts are to be *expected* for the welfare of the child. Jealous feelings on the part of a new spouse will no longer be tolerated. Here the concept of the business relationship is helpful in another way. **It is easier for your new spouse to accept your business relationship with your former partner than it is to accept a friendship.**

Finally, professionals helping step-families now know that those with younger children can eventually become more like a nuclear family than those with older children. These families have more years to develop closer attachments between step-parents and step-children. They also have less entrenched family rules and expectations when they come together in the first place, and it is easier to form new ways of relating.

The problems of families after second marriages are vast and very complex. Ideally, co-parents and step-parents will work together with acceptance and tolerance for the benefit of *all* the children. Those who are parenting both their own and another's children often have the most difficult jobs—and it will help if every adult involved will recognize this fact.

COMMITTED CO-PARENTS PREPARE TO SOLVE THEIR PROBLEMS

• **Part 4** LIVING THE CONCEPT OF COOPERATIVE PARENTING

In Part I we found that the acceptance of divorce is critical to the development of a successful co-parent relationship. Even after implementation of a sound parenting plan, you will need to work at cooperation. For many parents it is disheartening to find that in spite of their hard work they continue to worry and have problems.

Reading all of Part IV might help. The final points in the book will remind you that divorce is more a process than an event, and the process is never over. Your children and their needs should be constant reminders of the reason to keep your standards from becoming unrealistically high and of the reason to maintain your commitment.

STEP 14 ACCEPTING A LESS THAN PERFECT RESULT

No plan for co-parenting is flawless and no parent is perfect. Living in a post-divorce family requires enormous amounts of flexibility and tremendous energy for change. It also takes constant letting go of anger generated by the inevitable frustrations of trying to work together.

Even after you have recovered from your divorce, your old leanings toward blame and externalization may once again appear. These poor coping devices will be stumbling blocks to co-parenting. Now your *children* will suffer the most if your acceptance is incomplete.

Usually parents who are chronically upset after the specific plan is in force are still focusing on the negative aspects, or *possible negative aspects*, of the other parent's care of the child. Often this negative focus leads to distortions and false conclusions, with exaggerated anxiety about the child's welfare. Allegations of neglect and incompetence follow because regardless of the accuracy of one parent's perceptions they simply *seem* to be true. This error-prone way of responding becomes habitual to anxious, divorced parents. As a side effect it also destroys their efforts to parent cooperatively.

> Ah, when to the heart of man
> Was it ever less than a treason
> To go with the drift of things
> To yield with a grace to reason
> And bow and accept at the end
> Of a love or a season.
>
> Robert Frost

The simple technique of **re-framing,** adapted from cognitive therapy and introduced in Step 6, can help you develop the type of thinking that is the basis for co-parent acceptance. This tool will help you practice working through upsetting events without imposing heavy emotional judgements. The following common experiences describe certain typical *inflamed* responses that can spontaneously occur. Try to internalize the *neutral* responses rather than the overreactions:

Event

Your child returns from the other parent's home dirty and in need of a bath for the third time in a row.

Inflamed Response

You think your co-parent has not remembered to keep the child clean and therefore doesn't care.

Neutral Response

You consider that your co-parent's time with your child is limited, and there is always lots to do. You simply bathe the child.

Event

Your co-parent is chronically late when picking up the child, by as much as 15 minutes.

Inflamed Response

You think your ex-spouse is out to control you by making you wait, and you also think the child suffers greatly.

Neutral Response

You tell yourself that some individuals are always late. You downplay its intent and meaning. You and the child learn to expect the parent to be late and eliminate the wait as a problem.

Event

Your co-parent tells you the child is ill and cannot come to your home for a scheduled block of time. It seems this happens a lot.

Inflamed Response

You think your co-parent is willfully keeping the child from you.

Neutral Response

You tell yourself that children who are even slightly ill are less able to tolerate the stress of changing households. You let it go and reschedule the time.

The point of re-framing is not to overlook serious neglect, alienation, or withholding of the child. Its intent, rather, is to help you stop manufacturing problems that are not really there by substituting positive or neutral thoughts for negative ones. This strategy takes considerable effort on the part of individuals still healing from the wounds of spousal divorce. But it provides the committed mother's and father's most direct route to parental recovery.

Accepting a less-than-perfect result after the parenting plan is in effect means regaining control of your expectations — allowing yourself and your child to live life differently than you did before divorce became a reality. There are many ways for parents to take care of their children and many variations of acceptable parenting.

When co-parents cease projecting their own ideas and standards onto each other, they take a giant step toward their own well-being, as well as that of their children.

LETTING GO OF PARENTAL
JUDGEMENTS WILL HELP

STEP 15 GETTING HELP WHEN YOU NEED IT

Many post-divorce couples are either destined or determined to struggle in spite of their stated efforts to put the children first. Some of you are inclined to abandon the concept of working together and to just try "parallel" parenting. Others refuel the fiery battles of a custody change; still others withdraw or disengage completely. Unfortunately, all these developments can hurt your child by leading to further loss.

MEDIATION

"Alternative dispute resolution" first came about as a negotiation tool for employers and workers in industry. But mediation is a major contribution the business world has made to the welfare of families and children as well. Recently, its application to divorce and custody has been refined. Now mediators are available to parents in conflict almost everywhere.

Mediators are neutral, third party, helping professionals who facilitate agreements between parents. They may be trained in child development, psychology, law, or a combination of these disciplines. They follow specific procedures and rules of communication, such as those presented in Step 7. Mediators help parents create parenting plans, frequently using a checklist similar to the one in Appendix A.

Parents should plan to consider mediation from the outset of their separation if there are areas of serious parental disagreement. The process of organized conflict resolution will help you solve your problems without hurting your children. You should go to mediation whenever you reach an impasse in your ability to agree, before or after your divorce is final.

Families who cannot afford a mediator or who live in rural areas where none is available should find a mediator-substitute when they need one. This neutral person can help co-parents in the same general way, even without the professional background. Often a friend or trusted relative would be happy to try. Parenting seminars and support groups are also starting to appear; these resources may prove helpful in locating volunteer lay-mediators.

Cooperative parents should never let feelings of embarrassment or humiliation keep them from asking for help. Bear in mind that your child's well-being is at stake, and continuing conflict is destructive. **Mothers and fathers who truly understand the concept of co-parenting continue to view each other as important to the child's development, and they show this in their endless attempts to resolve their difficulties.**

THERAPY

Co-parents, as business partners, should use the services of a mediator when there are serious disagreements about caring for the children. But mediation is not intended to address the emotional aspects of either parent's personal functioning, and it does not include the child directly at all. For these kinds of problems, counseling or individual therapy is still best.

Life demands compromise and half-solutions.
Theodor Reik, psychoanalyst

WHEN ADULTS NEED HELP

Adults need personal therapeutic help when one of two situations develops:

1. The grieving and sadness is so painful that support will help during the worst period of divorce crisis.

2. The grieving is denied and not worked through normally. Only anger, blame, and conflict prevail, well past the period of initial crisis.

In the first case the role of the counselor is to help you work through the stages of mourning more easily. In the second case, however, the role of the professional is much greater. Here the therapist must facilitate a break-through in your emotional block to help you move beyond denial and projection.

This second type of treatment must be more confrontational and direct than the former supportive counseling, so it may be harder for you to accept. However, hurting divorcees sometimes spend months venting angry feelings to accommodating listeners who do little to jar their distorted views. In these cases nothing seems to improve. If this is your experience, what you need instead is to interact with a professional who will help you face your own issues more directly, gently teaching you to tolerate your painful feelings of loss.

Reviewing Parts I and II of this manual may help parents who cannot move on. Reading the Books Recommended for Parents in the References may also help. For many of you, however, one-to-one or group therapy from a qualified divorce psychotherapist is the only thing that will work.

WHEN CHILDREN NEED HELP

Children often need special help after divorce, but not in every case. Child symptoms and indications for treatment can be divided into three levels of severity:

1. Mild Grief Reactions: Signs of distress are obvious but short-lived. The symptoms are expected and understandable. Younger children show sadness, fear, separation anxiety, and eating or sleep disturbances. Older children show discipline problems, become angry, and want to control others. Sometimes they withdraw. Normal grief reactions may last from several weeks to one year.

Only a few children with mild grief reactions need professional help. Most children are able to adjust by working through their feelings with the help of their parents. Signs of unhappiness go away as the re-structured family becomes familiar.

2. Prolonged Grief Reactions: When symptoms do not disappear, parents become more concerned. The signs of prolonged distress for younger children are the same as when situational grief occurs, but they seem to get worse, not better. Older children may begin to blame the parents, refuse to transfer from home to home, and act out their grief in social settings.

Children with prolonged grief reactions may or may not need professional help. The source of the problem may be that poor decisions have been made in setting up the parenting plan. A young child given an inappropriate time-share schedule will manifest ongoing problems until the errors are corrected. Making the right change in routine will alleviate stress right away.

Some children with moderate signs of distress benefit from individual counseling; others need family therapy. An especially sensitive child unusually saddened by separation will feel better after talking with a trained adult who understands. But another, who confuses his or her own grief with the parent's mourning, shows faster progress when one or both parents participate in therapy. Here a counselor helps separate the child's pain from that of the mother or father, making it possible for each family member to progress.

> Something it is which thou hast lost,
> Some pleasure from thine early years.
> Break, thou deep vase of chilling tears
> That grief hath shaken into frost!
> Alfred Lord Tennyson

3. Extreme Chronic Reactions: These symptoms clearly represent more than normal grief. They are the child's signs of distress caused by witnessing, or being part of, ongoing high conflict between parents. Younger children blame themselves, talk about dying, have nightmares, and often cannot eat. They are extremely fearful and insecure in many ways. Older children have serious problems with their emotions, behavior, or learning. Some develop problems with substance abuse and become impossible to control. They refuse to go along with time-sharing or they even run away.

All children who show extreme chronic reactions to divorce need professional help. In these cases, both individual and family therapy are called for. The child's internal world is admittedly deeply troubled, but the external world involving parents has become chaotic as well. **Nearly all seriously troubled children are taking cues from their unhappy parents.**

Tending to a child's emotional disturbance in the most serious instance will take a skilled family therapist. This professional will treat the child individually and also guide the parents toward a healthier family structure. Effective child specialists encourage parents to achieve a better working relationship and to cease putting their own needs before those of their children.

If this kind of intense treatment is still ineffective, the real problem in the re-structured world of the child is one or both parents' inability to progress beyond personal anger. Though at times it may be difficult for mothers or fathers to accept, children sometimes are best served when suffering parents enter personal counseling themselves. When mediation, child counseling, and even family therapy do not work, parents should consider individual therapy for themselves.

COMMITTED CO-PARENTS GET PROFESSIONAL HELP WHEN THEY NEED IT

STEP 16 KEEPING THE COMMITMENT TO CO-PARENTING

VISUALIZING YOUR FUTURE

At the beginning of this book we described a hypothetical scenario about your family to illustrate the trauma of divorce. The sequence began with a dream-like visualization of you on your wedding day. It encompassed your hope for a happy home and your wishes for a permanent family life, which included children.

Later, when you were struck by the reality of divorce, your dream-like image was shattered, replaced by pain and suffering. You were unable to identify joys or hopes about your future—only grief about what was gone and the split images of your family.

But once you have recovered from the parent- divorce, you begin to dream again, and the future looks much brighter. Dream, and dream you should, for visualizing happiness in this way will help you set new goals and family objectives. When you can imagine your children growing up—moving through adult life-stages—and when you are able to see yourself in the picture, you know you are on the way.

> I don't know anyone who has got to the top without hard work. That is the recipe. It will not always get you to the top, but should get you pretty near.
>
> Margaret Thatcher

As you begin to adjust and look toward the future, your visions will be more true-to-life than they once were. Now you know reality. Now you know that you will only *sometimes* have your child near you, and you will only *sometimes* be in charge. Many times your co-parent and other adults will be there, caring for and enjoying your child. Step-parents, step-siblings, half-siblings, and networks of partially related cousins or in-laws may appear in the scenarios you imagine.

The happiness you visualize after successful recovery from the parental divorce readily includes these extended and blended family members. They will be present at the recitals, communions, bar miztvahs, graduations, and weddings of your children. There will be pictures of them in your child's family album. Earlier, these expectations were entirely unimaginable, but now you accept them, even embrace them, for your child's sake and for your own.

Congratulations on your progress!

RECOGNIZING THE JOYS OF HARMONY

Once they have achieved acceptance, parents wanting to keep the peace should verbalize their positive emotions with self-talk. They should tell each other they feel better. Together they should validate each other's efforts and express mutual gratification that things have truly improved. They should use the forum of the co-parent meeting to *thank each other* for concessions that have been made. Every business person likes to have a positive job review, and parents as business partners are no different.

Capitalizing on the coalition when it is good can also help former spouses plan for more difficult times in the family growth process. If you and your former spouse are experiencing times of peace, you should talk about how you will always work at shared parenting as your family network changes. Harmonious moments are most conducive to refining your philosophies on post-divorce child-rearing.

A final point is that years of pleasant times with your child will follow if you allow accord to continue. Sometimes disagreement has become so familiar that conflict is equated with normalcy. Then divorcing parents feel uncomfortable when strife and fighting have finally subsided. What follows is a quest to find imperfection with parenting arrangements, and again, the peace is jeopardized.

Real recovery from the parent-divorce means working through the stages of grief to arrive at genuine acceptance. When the journey is finally over, divorced parents can revel in their accomplishments. They will have arrived at new-found freedom for themselves, and they can count the blessings for their children. Their loved ones will have been given an invaluable gift. Parents really are forever when children, mothers, and fathers can dream together.

Every child, dependent as he is on the help of the community, finds himself face to face with a world that gives and takes, that expects adoption and satisfies life. His instincts are baffled in their fulfillment by obstacles whose conquest gives him pain. His soul is born, one might say, in those situations of childhood which demand an organ of integration, whose function is to make a normal life possible.

Alfred Adler, psychoanalyst

Appendix A   Co-Parent Checklist

ISSUES	DECISIONS
Legal Custody	
Residential or Physical Custody	
Parent Time-Share Routine	
Holidays and Birthdays	
Vacations	

Daycare

Transportation

Policy for
Rearranging
Parenting Time

Medical
Decisions

School
Decisions

Religious
Upbringing

Child Support

Medical Costs	
Community Activities	
Telephone Calls	
Shopping for Clothing	
Items to be Duplicated	
Items to be Shared	
Information to be Exchanged Between Parents	

Grandparent Visits	
Involvement With Other Adults	
How Changes in Time Share Will be Made	
Consistency Between Households	
Supporting the Other Parent	
Communicating With the Other Parent	
Controlling Conflict	

Provisions for
Mediation

Geographical
Moves

Provisions for
Higher Education

Other Matters

Appendix B

We, the parties of this separation, are in agreement that the welfare of our son, age 7, and our daughter, age 5, will be best served if we maintain a harmonious and cooperative parenting relationship. Each of us acknowledges the loving concern of the other and pledges to create an environment wherein our children will have access to both of us. To this end, we have made the agreements below:

❏ **Legal Custody.**   After considering all legal custody alternatives, we have decided that our children's interest will be best served with joint legal custody. We will consult each other and make joint decisions on all matters that seriously affect our children.

❏ **Residential Custody.** In addition to our agreement regarding legal custody of our children, we have decided that the best primary and non-primary residential assignments will be: The primary residence of our son and daughter will be with mother, and the non-primary residence will be with father. We further agree to review the primary/non-primary residential needs of each child yearly and to make necessary changes of the living arrangements as our children grow.

❏ **Routine Parent Time-Share.** Father will have parenting time with our son every other Thursday from 6 p.m. until Sunday 6 p.m. Father will have parenting time with our daughter every other Friday from 6 p.m. until Sunday 6 p.m., to coincide with her brother's weekends with father. Additional one-on-one time for father with our son will be every Tuesday from 5 p.m. until 7 p.m. and for father with our daughter every Wednesday from 5 p.m. until 7 p.m. We agree to prepare detailed calendars outlining the routine parenting time blocks for each of us and to share the calendars with our children. Holidays and vacation time as indicated in sections below will be included on the calendar.

❒ **Holidays and Birthdays.** We agree to share holidays and our children's birthdays in the following way:

Mother will have holiday and parenting time with the children from 8 a.m. until 8 p.m. on the following holidays beginning the season of our separation and every other year thereafter: New Year's Day, Memorial Day, Labor Day, Thanksgiving, Christmas Eve, and our son's birthday. Mother will always spend Mother's Day with the children.

Father will have holiday and parenting time with the children from 8 a.m. until 8 p.m. on the following holidays beginning the season after the year of our separation and every other year thereafter: Easter, Independence Day, Halloween, Christmas Day, and our daughter's birthday. Father will always spend Father's Day with the children. We agree to be flexible in rearranging these special times with our children as may be necessary over the years.

❒ **Vacations.** We agree that vacation time for our children with each of us will be important. We will plan our vacations no later than Memorial Day each summer, and will trade itineraries so as to maintain communication beneficial to our children.

❒ **Day Care.** Each of us agrees to do the majority of caretaking of our children when we have parenting time and to invite the other to care for the children when we need help. When outside day care is necessary, we will try to seek caretakers that are mutually acceptable.

❒ **Transportation.** We agree to share in the transportation of our children as follows: Mother will deliver the children to father's home at the beginning of his parenting time. Father will deliver the children to mother's home at the end of his parenting time.

❒ **Policy for Cancelling/Rescheduling Time-Share.** We agree to change our parenting time schedule as infrequently as possible. In the event that changes need to be made, we agree to request of each other such change at least 14 days in advance. We understand that requests may need to be refused from time to time. When our children are sick during a scheduled block of parenting time, this time will be made up as soon as possible.

❒ **Medical and School Decisions.** We agree to share medical and school decision-making. We also agree to share information with each other, including reports from doctors and teachers. We agree that it will be in our children's best interest for both of us to attend school activities and to be courteous with each other on these occasions.

❒ **Religious Upbringing.** We agree that father will involve the children in the Christian religion and provide religious training during his parenting time.

❒ **Child Support.** We agree to follow customary guidelines in deciding each parent's financial obligation to our children. Payments will be made by the 15th day of each month unless extraordinary circumstances occur.

❒ **Medical Costs.** We agree that the parent most able to maintain adequate health insurance for our children will do so. Father will maintain the policy currently in effect for the time being. Medical costs not covered by the policy will be divided equally between us and reconciled with each other on a monthly basis.

❒ **Community Activities.** We agree to communicate with each other about which activities are best for our children. We will schedule activities on our own time, and avoid those that interfere with the other's parenting time. We agree to provide each other with all pertinent calendars and schedules of sports activities and special events.

❒ **Telephone Calls.** Our children may have free access to each of us by telephone. We will limit our own calls to the children when they are in the other home, however, calling only once during a weekend block of parenting time.

❒ **Shopping and Setting Up Households.** We agree that mother will provide most of the clothing for our children and that father will be responsible for purchasing winter coats on a yearly basis, as well as sports uniforms for each child. We agree that each of us will cooperate in sharing and returning the children's clothing to the other home as necessary. Each of us will provide the children toiletries in our home.

❑ **Sharing Parental Information.** We agree to keep each other informed of our own permanent and temporary addresses and telephone numbers, and of our vacation itineraries. We acknowledge that this agreement is for the welfare of our children so that necessary communication is possible. We pledge not to intrude unnecessarily into each other's personal lives.

❑ **Involvement with Other Adults.** We agree to exercize good judgement and use discretion in bringing other adults into our children's lives.

❑ **Grandparent Visits.** We acknowledge the importance of the loving relationships our children have with their all their grandparents. We agree to provide for grandparenting time on our own vacation time and whenever maternal or paternal grandparents visit our community.

❑ **Changing the Time-Share Routine.** We agree that our childrens' needs for parenting time with each of us may change as they grow. We agree to have regular co-parent meetings at least twice yearly until our youngest child is seven years of age, and yearly after that. The purpose of the meetings will be to review our childrens' needs, and to restructure parenting time if it will benefit either child.

❑ **Consistency of Households.** We agree that it is best for our children if we maintain similar standards of living. We agree to support each other in our parenting roles and to discuss general rules and expectations for our children.

❑ **Handling Conflict.** We agree to maintain positive communication for the sake of our children. Should conflict arise, we agree to curtail overt anger immediately. We agree that we will never argue or criticize each other in front of our children, but we will schedule co-parent meetings to discuss our problems.

❑ **Mediation.** We agree to retain the services of a professional mediator to help resolve serious problems and to share the cost of mediation equally.

❐ **Geographical Moves.** We agree that it is in our childrens' best interest to reside within driving distance of each other so that frequent time-sharing is possible. In the event either of us finds it necessary to consider a move that prevents frequent time-sharing, we will discuss the move with the other parent prior to finalizing the decision and assure that an appropriate long-distance parenting plan has been determined.

❐ **Higher Education.** We acknowledge the importance and value of post high school education for our children. We agree that we will share in the cost of attaining a bachelor's degree or technical training certificate if our son or daughter chooses such an educational experience.

❐ **Other Agreements.**

_____

Mother's Signature   Date

_____

Father's Signature   Date

References

* Books Recommended for Parents

* Ahrons, Constance R., *The Good Divorce*, Harper Collins, New York, 1994.

* Baris, Mitchell A. and Garrity, Carla B., *Children of Divorce*, Psytec, DeKalb, IL, 1988.

* Blau, Melinda. *Families Apart*, G. P. Putnam's Sons, New York, 1993.

Bray, James H., "What's In The Best Interest of the Child? Children's Adjustment Issues in Divorce," *The Independent Practitioner*, Vol. 13, #1, pp. 42-45, 1993.

Depner, C. and Bray, J., eds., *Nonresidential Parenting: New Vistas in Family Living*, Sage Publications, Newbury Park, CA, 1993.

Emery, Robert E., *Renegotiating Family Relationships*, Guilford, New York, 1994.

* Fisher, Bruce, *When Your Relationship Ends*, Impact Publishers, San Luis Obispo, CA, 1981.

Fitzgerald, Helen, *The Grieving Child, A Parent' Guide*, Fireside, New York, 1992.

Garrity, Carla B. and Baris, Mitchell A., *Caught in the Middle*, Lexington Books, New York, 1994.

Gardner, Richard A., *Child Custody Litigation: A Guide for Parents and Mental Health Professionals*, Creative Therapeutics, New Jersey, 1986.

Gardner, Richard A., *The Parental Alienation Syndrome and the Differentiation Between Fabricated and Genuine Child Sex Abuse*, Creative Therapeutics, New Jersey, 1987.

Goldstein, Joseph; Freud, Anna; and Solnit, Albert J., *Before the Best Interests of the Child*, The Free Press, New York, 1979.

Gottman, John; Notarius, Cliff; Gonso, Jonni; and Markman, Howard, *A Couple's Guide to Communication*, Research Press, Champaigne, IL, 1976.

Hodges, William, *Interventions for Children of Divorce,* Wiley and Sons, New York, 1986.

Hodges, William, *Interventions for Children of Divorce, Book II*, Wiley & Sons, New York, 1991.

Jaffe, Peter G.; Wolfe, David A.; and Wilson, Susan Kaye, *Children of Battered Women,* Sage Publications, Newbury Park, CA, 1990.

* Johnson, Laurene and Rosenfeld, Georglyn, *Divorced Kids*, Faucett Crest, New York, 1979.

Johnston, Janet R. and Campbell, Linda E. G., *Impasses of Divorce*, Free Press, New York, 1988.

* Kalter, Neil, *Growing Up With Divorce*, Free Press, New York, 1990.

Kelly, Joan, "The Adjustment of Children After Divorce: Are Negative Effects Exaggerated?" *Family Law News*, 15, No. 1, 1992.

* Kline, Kris and Pew, Stephen, *For the Sake of the Children*, Prima Publishing, Rocklin, CA, 1992.

Kubler-Ross, Elisabeth, *On Death and Dying*, MacMillan, New York, 1969.

Levy, David, ed., *The Best Parent is Both Parents: A Guide to Shared Parenting in the 21st Century,* Hampton Roads, Norfolk, VA, 1993.

* Marston, Stephanie, *The Divorced Parent,* Morrow & Company, Inc., New York, 1994.

* Ricci, Isolina, *Mom's House, Dad's House: Making Shared Custody Work*, Macmillan, New York, 1980.

Taylor, Alison, "Shared Parenting: What it takes to Succeed," *Joint Custody: Shared Parenting*, Jay Folberg, ed., Guilford, New York, 1991.

* Teyber, Edward, *Helping Children Cope With Divorce*, Lexington Books, New York, 1992.

Wallerstein, Judith S. and Blakeslee, Sandra, *Second Chances: Men, Women, and Children a Decade After Divorce, Who Wins, Who Loses, and Why*, Ticknor & Fields, New York, 1990.

Weisinger, Hendrie, *Dr. Weisinger's Anger Work Out Book*, Quill, New York, 1985.